Hallett, Harold F.
Benedict de Spinoza

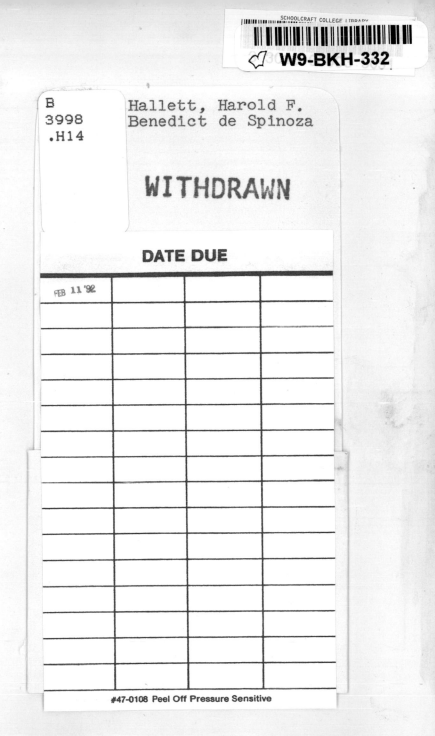

DATE DUE

FEB 11 '92			

#47-0108 Peel Off Pressure Sensitive

BENEDICT DE SPINOZA

BENEDICT DE SPINOZA

THE ELEMENTS OF HIS PHILOSOPHY

by

H. F. HALLETT

M.A., D.LITT.

Professor Emeritus of Philosophy
in the University of London

UNIVERSITY OF LONDON
THE ATHLONE PRESS
1957

Published by
THE ATHLONE PRESS
UNIVERSITY OF LONDON
at 2 Gower Street, London, W.C.1
Distributed by Constable & Co. Ltd
12 Orange Street, London, W.C.2

Canada
University of Toronto Press
Toronto, 5

U.S.A.
Essential Books Inc
Fair Lawn, New Jersey

Printed in Great Britain by
WESTERN PRINTING SERVICES LTD
BRISTOL

Every discourse, once written, is bandied about both among those who understand it and those for whom it is in no wise fitted; and it does not know to whom it ought, and to whom it ought not, to speak. And when misunderstood and unjustly attacked it needs its author to help it, for unaided it can neither retaliate nor defend itself.

PLATO, *Phaedrus*, 275

PREFACE

Probably no philosopher of repute has been worse served by his expositors and commentators than Spinoza. Monist, pantheist, atheist, acosmist, ethical nihilist, mechanist, mystic, and even dialectical materialist, are among the epithets more or less commonly used to describe and pigeon-hole a doctrine which, nevertheless, though neglected, misinterpreted, and deplored, has never been despised as a mere curiosity of philosophical history. Thinkers as disparate as Hegel and Bergson have regarded Spinoza as the 'philosopher's philosopher', and the recollection of him operates as a sort of 'conscience' from which philosophers, however alien in thought, and critically disposed, can never feel wholly 'safe'. This, doubtless, is in part due to Spinoza's reputation for intellectual candour and disinterestedness, but also, and perhaps even more, to the haunting suspicion that essential clues to the solution of world-problems are still to be discovered if the 'eyes of the mind' can be brought to see by the aid of the intellectual lenses that he so assiduously polished in the pages of the *Ethics* and elsewhere.

But there is no easy way by which these aids may be acquired. Certainly, Spinoza is not to be understood by those who, avoiding his admittedly difficult texts, turn to the inadequate and eccentric interpretations of writers who, by reason of their own presuppositions, derived from schools of thought alien to Spinoza—presuppositions that they have not had the intellectual detachment to correct—cannot but fail to present an account adequate to the profundity of his thought, or even, as in many cases, to do elementary justice to his philosophical sagacity and plain sense. For it is not easy for the modern mind, steeped as it is in empiricistic modes of thought subsequently developed, to take up the intellectual standpoint from which alone the thought of Spinoza is intelligible. Yet, of course, until this has been accomplished, exposition and criticism alike are futile.

Of no philosopher is it more true to say, than of Spinoza, that it is from a careful study of his own words, avoiding a too-great readiness in the early stages to draw conclusions that he does not himself draw—conclusions that are often but the offspring of pre-suppositions alien or even anachronistic—that true profit is likely to accrue to the serious student. Yet this is to ask not a little, both by way of caution and by way of persistence, for many of his key-terms have subsequently gathered an alien connotation, and his literary style is in general dry, laconic, and in form (though not in significance) abstract and *prima facie* forbidding to those who take pleasure in the plain commonsense of a Locke, the easy charm of a Berkeley, the sub-humorous ingenuousness of a Hume, or the analogical fertility of a Bacon, a Schopenhauer, or a Bergson. Not that he cannot on occasion write with simplicity, clarity, and verve; but in general, earnestness and concentration, with a certain detachment, suppress the man in the interests of the doctrine.

Though the treatment of its subject is relatively brief, and in its way 'popular' as avoiding over-elaboration and textual detail, this book is intended for the use of the candid student, and not for 'the man in the train'. It is devised as a monitory preparation for deeper study of the philosophy of Spinoza. By its means it is hoped that the student may avoid the chief pitfalls of Spinoza-interpretation, and be carried past many of the difficulties encountered by the modern mind in the study of his writings. To this end perhaps the greatest hindrance to be met by the beginner is the 'popular' exposition that attempts to expound the thought of one age in terms of the favoured categories of another. By providing the necessary safeguards against misinterpretations arising from such causes (not absent, it is to be feared, even from the classical expositions available to the student), I have sought to awaken interest in the closely knit fabric of Spinoza's doctrine of man and nature and God, and its practical import—and thus to revivify a specimen too long deprived of its native air.

Something ought, perhaps, to be added here concerning the sources of the portrait of Spinoza that I have ventured to include. Our knowledge of the outward physical appearance of the philosopher, though not to be compared with that which is available concerning his inward mind, is tolerably authentic. It is derived from the brief descriptions of his earliest biographers and from four contemporary drawings. According to the former, 'he was of medium build, his features well proportioned, his complexion dark, his hair black and curly, his eyebrows long and of the same colour, so that one might easily know that he was descended from Portuguese Jews'; 'his expression was very genial, and held one unconsciously'; 'his clothes were no better than those of the meanest citizen', yet 'there was that something about his dress that usually distinguishes a gentleman from a pedant'. As to the drawings, though at a casual glance their differences may suggest not merely bad portraiture but even false identification, yet more careful and prolonged scrutiny does much to dispel these doubts. The engraving contained in some copies of the *Opera Posthuma* and the Wolfenbüttel oil-painting (whichever may be the prior) are plainly versions of the same; and the small juvenile portrait of 1660, if due allowance is made for the youthful beard and cropped hair, reveals certain fundamental agreements with the latter, which is certainly of a Sephardic Jew. This, too, is emphasized by, and would explain, the old-fashioned Spanish costume. Perhaps the so-called 'Van der Spyck' miniature is the least convincing from its too young and well-favoured air of somewhat garrulous humour; yet (as is evinced by the interestingly faded photograph of it reproduced by E. Altkirch as frontispiece to his *Spinoza im Porträt* (Jena, 1913)) this may well be due only to over-elaboration and emphasis on his reputed geniality of expression. Thus I have allowed even this portrait to influence my attempted pictorial eirenicon.

It only remains for me to acknowledge with gratitude the generous help I have received from my friend Professor A. E. Teale who read the whole in typescript, and promoted some important emendations.

H. F. H.

CONTENTS

Part I

THE DOCTRINE OF BEING

Part II

THE DOCTRINE OF KNOWLEDGE

Part III

THE DOCTRINE OF LIBERATION

BIOGRAPHICAL NOTE

Benedictus de Spinoza (Baruch Despinoza) was born at Amsterdam on 24 November 1632, of a family of refugee Jews from the Peninsula, probably (though 'Espinoza' is also a Spanish place-name) more immediately from Portugal. Brought up as an orthodox Sephardic Jew, he received the customary training in letters and Talmudic theology. His people entertained high hopes for his future, but he appears to have become increasingly critical in outlook, and irregular in ritual observance, and was at last formally excommunicated by the Amsterdam synagogue in 1656. About this time he left Amsterdam and lived, first at Ouwerkerk, a village near by, and after 1660 at Rijnsburg in the vicinity of Leyden, associating with Mennonites and members of the anti-clerical Christian community of Collegiants, the headquarters of which was in the latter place. He now devoted himself to intellectual and scientific pursuits, earning his living by the manufacture of optical lenses for telescopes and microscopes. Our knowledge of his life and character is mainly derived from two early biographies: that of his near contemporary J. M. Lucas (see A. Wolf, *The Oldest Biography of Spinoza*), and that of J. Köhler (Colerus) published in 1706 (see F. Pollock, *Spinoza, His Life and Philosophy*, Appendix). He had learned, and perhaps also taught, Latin at the school of the free-thinking F. A. van den Ende, and he was evidently much impressed, and his originality stimulated, by the 'new philosophy' of Descartes. His character comes down to us as that of a man devoted to the search after truth, and wholly disinterested in its pursuit, who gradually won a wide reputation both among his associates and also in the general republic of letters. From his writings also we can safely judge that sobriety, piety, and mental acuity were with him untinged by asceticism, bigotry, and pedantry; and, man of letters, and something of a hermit, as he was, he yet took a keen interest in public affairs. In the early years after his excommunication he appears to have been a prominent member of a philosophical discussion group, and it has been surmised that the MSS. later discovered and published as the *Short Treatise on God, Man, and His Wellbeing* were connected with this activity. His earliest published work, and the only one openly bearing his name, however, was the *Geometrical Version of Descartes's Principles of Philosophy* (with its Appendix of *Metaphysical Reflections* tacitly providing many a spinozistic gloss on the main work), which had its origin in some lessons he had given to a fellow-lodger. This was published in 1663, and was probably influential in gaining for him in 1673 an invitation from the Elector Palatine to the Chair of Philosophy at Heidelberg—and that in spite of the clamour produced by

his second published work, the *Tractatus Theologico-Politicus* which had
first appeared anonymously in 1670, but was already generally ascribed to
him. Spinoza, however, preferred to continue the life of a private and
independent scholar. In 1663 he had removed to Voorburg, near The
Hague, where the latter work was completed; and in the year of its publication finally moved to The Hague, lodging after 1671 in the house by
the Pavilion Canal which is now dedicated to his memory. Here the *Ethics*
was completed and prepared for publication. News of this having got
abroad, and garbled accounts of its nature rumoured, he decided to with-
hold publication, fearing a renewal of the clamour raised by the *Tractatus
Theologico-Politicus*—arranging with his printer in Amsterdam that in
case of his death before a more favourable occasion should arise this work,
together with his other literary remains, should then be brought to light.
Though he was in poor health from the increasing inroads of phthisis, he
died without other warning in the presence of his doctor alone on 21 Feb-
ruary 1677. His posthumous works duly appeared in the same year.

BIBLIOGRAPHICAL NOTE

WORKS

Renati Des Cartes Principiorum Philosophiae Pars. I. et II., More Geometrico Demonstratae per Benedictum de Spinoza Amstelodamensem. Accesserunt Ejusdem Cogitata Metaphysica, Amstelodami, 1663.
Tractatus Theologico-Politicus, Hamburgi, MDCLXX.
Opera Posthuma, MDCLXXVII [N.P.]:
    I. *Ethica, More Geometrico Demonstrata.*
    II. *Tractatus Politicus.*
    III. *Tractatus de Intellectus Emendatione.*
    IV. *Epistolae, et ad eas Responsiones.*
    V. *Compendium Grammatices Linguae Hebraeae.*
Korte Verhandeling van God de Mensch en des Zelfs Welstand, Amstelodami, 1862.
Stelkonstige Reeckening van den Regenboog, 's Gravenhage, MDCLXXXVII.
Reeckening van Kanssen, Hagae Comitum, MDCCCLXXXII.

CHIEF COLLECTED EDITIONS

Benedicti de Spinoza Opera quae supersunt omnia. Ed. C. H. Bruder. 3 vols., *Lipsiae,* 1843–6. Vol. IV. *Supplementum.* Ed. J. van Vloten, *Amstelodami,* 1862.
Benedicti de Spinoza Opera quotquot reperta sunt. Ed. J. van Vloten et J. P. N. Land. *Hagae Comitum, MDCCCLXXXII–III.* 2 vols. *Editio altera,* 3 vols, *MDCCCVC. Editio tertia,* 4 (or 2) vols. *MCMXIII–IV.*
Spinoza Opera. Herausgegeben von Carl Gebhardt. Heidelberg, N.D. [1924], 4 vols.

ENGLISH TRANSLATIONS

Tractatus Theologico-Politicus. Trans. anonymous. London, 1862.
Benedict de Spinoza, His Life, Correspondence, and Ethics. By R. Willis, London, 1870.
The Chief Works of Benedict de Spinoza. 2 vols. (*Bohn's Philosophical Library*). Trans. R. H. M. Elwes. London, (from) 1883–4. (Containing: Vol. I. *Tract. Theo.-Pol., Tract. Polit.*; Vol. 2. *Tract. de Intell. Emend., Ethica,* and abridged Correspondence.)
Ethic Demonstrated in Geometrical Order. Trans. W. Hale White. London, 1883. Revised by A. Hutchison Stirling, 1899.
Tractatus de Intellectus Emendatione. Trans. W. Hale White. London, 1895. Revised by A. Hutchison Stirling, 1899.
Ethics and Treatise on the Correction of the Understanding. (*Everyman's Library*). Trans. A. Boyle. London, (from) 1910.

Spinoza's Short Treatise on God, Man, and His Wellbeing. Trans. A. Wolf. London, 1910.
The Correspondence of Spinoza. Trans. A. Wolf. London, 1928.
Spinoza on Descartes. Trans. H. F. Hallett and G. Brown. (Containing the *Descartes's Principles, Metaphysical Reflections*, etc.). [Ready for publication.]

OTHER WORKS

A discreet and critical use of some of the following selected studies may be of value or interest to the student:

Matthew Arnold, *Essays in Criticism, First Series*: Spinoza and the Bible. London, 1865.
J. A. Froude, *Short Stories on Great Subjects, First Series*: Spinoza. London, 1867.
F. Pollock, *Spinoza, His Life and Philosophy*. London, 1880. Second edition, 1899.
W. A. Knight (edit.), *Spinoza, Four Essays*. London, 1882.
J. Martineau, *A Study of Spinoza*. London, 1882.
H. H. Joachim, *A Study of the Ethics of Spinoza*. Oxford, 1901.
— *Spinoza's* Tractatus de Intellectus Emendatione. *A Commentary*. Oxford, 1940.
R. A. Duff, *Spinoza's Political and Ethical Philosophy*. Glasgow, 1903.
G. Huan, *Le Dieu de Spinoza*. Paris, 1914.
V. Delbos, *Le Spinozisme*. Paris, 1916.
E. Lasbax, *La Hiérarchie dans l'Univers chez Spinoza*. Paris, 1919.
L. Brunschvicg, *Spinoza et ses Contemporains*. Paris, 1923.
R. Lévêque, *Le Problème de la Verité dans la Philosophie de Spinoza*. Strasbourg, 1923.
L. Roth, *Spinoza, Descartes, and Maimonides*. London, 1924.
— *Spinoza* (Leaders of Philosophy Series). London, 1929.
A. Guzzo, *Il pensiero di B. Spinoza*. Florence, 1924.
J. Freudenthal, *Spinoza's Leben und Lehre* (Bibliotheca Spinozana, Vol. V, ed. C. Gebhardt). Heidelberg, 1927.
L. Robinson, *Kommentar zu Spinozas Ethik*. Leipzig, 1928.
R. McKeon, *The Philosophy of Spinoza*. New York, 1928.
H. F. Hallett, Aeternitas, *A Spinozistic Study*. Oxford, 1930.
— *Creation, Emanation, and Salvation, Another Spinozistic Study*. [Ready for publication.]
D. Bidney, *The Psychology and Ethics of Spinoza*. Newhaven, Conn., 1940.
G. H. R. Parkinson, *Spinoza's Theory of Knowledge*. Oxford, 1954.
Chronicon Spinozanum. 5 vols., Spinoza Society, The Hague, 1921–27.
W. G. de Burgh, 'Great Thinkers (VIII): Spinoza' (*Philosophy* xi, 1936, pp. 271–87).
F. Kaufmann, 'Spinoza's System as Theory of Expression' (*Philos. and Phenomenolog. Research*, 1940, pp. 83–97).
H. Barker, 'Notes on the Second Part of Spinoza's *Ethics*' (*Mind*, N.S. xlvii, 1948, pp. 159–79, 281–302, 417–39).

INTRODUCTION

It is not easy for the modern mind, steeped as it is in the sophistical heresies of a truncated empiricistic philosophy that confines its attention to the objective accidents of experience, ignoring its prime essence, as well as the activity by which alone the objects of experience can be distinguished from those objective accidents, to take up the intellectual standpoint from which alone the thought of Spinoza is intelligible. For the prime essence of experience lies, not in the extrinsic objects experienc*ed*, but in the intrinsic active experienc*ing* as modalized by its objective accidents. There is nothing in the philosophy of Spinoza to exclude an empiricism which takes due account of all these factors of experience—indeed, the 'analytic' method necessarily begins with extant imperfect human experience, and proceeds by emendation of this towards a perfected knowledge of first principles. This is the burden of the analogy[1] which he draws between the making of physical tools, such as a hammer, and the search after truth. Since a hammer is needed in order to forge a hammer, unless nature provided man with crude hammers the forging of iron would be impossible, and man could never be provided with perfected tools. So also the intellect of man must be provided by nature with crude apprehensions, so that 'by its own native force' it can 'form for itself intellectual tools' of increasing perfection, and by degrees advance towards perfected apprehension. It is true that in the *Ethics* his philosophy is expounded, in the main, not analytically but synthetically 'in the geometrical manner', beginning from first principles rather than from crude human apprehensions; but those first principles, though implicit in experience as such, have been made explicit by the analysis and emendation of crude apprehension; and the reversed synthetic order does but accommodate human discovery with the order of nature, i.e. with the order of creation. For analysis and emenda-

---

[1] *Tract. de Intell. Emend.*, §§ 30–1.

B

tion there is now substituted analogy and synthesis, the imperfect objects of crude experience being more adequately recognized as more or less imperfect expressions of that perfect being that is the essential object of intellect. For Spinoza, therefore, *analytical* metaphysical method is not from an empirical basis by *ascending analogy* to perfected knowledge, but by the *emendation* of crude experience; and *synthetical* metaphysical method is not the mere *reversal* of the analytical order (which could only bring us back to crude experience) but a movement by *descending analogy* from first principles to adequate knowledge of the real nature of the objects of crude experience as finite and privative expressions of infinite exemplary being. And human finiteness entails imperfection in both movements: the results of analysis being necessarily abstract, and those of synthesis no more than approximate. Man's idea of God or *Natura* is adequate but not exhaustive; his ideas of empirical things analogical rather than incorrigibly direct.

It must not be thought, however, that Spinoza was occupied as a philosopher solely in the intellectual clarification of experience. The moving force of his investigations in this sphere was the impulse to discover the way of human salvation, and the principles of the good life for man. The term 'Ethics' as the title of his central metaphysical work correctly indicates this main purpose which the opening paragraphs of the *Tractatus de Intellectus Emendatione* had openly expressed: 'After experience had taught me that all the things commonly met with in ordinary life are vain and futile . . . I at length determined to inquire whether . . . there was anything by the discovery and acquisition of which I might be put in possession of a joy continuous and supreme for eternity. . . . I saw that I was situated in the greatest peril, and pulled myself together to seek with all my power a remedy . . . just as a sick man suffering from a mortal disease, who foresees certain death unless a remedy be applied, is forced to seek it with all his strength, even though it be uncertain.'[1] There is more than a touch of Bunyan's Pilgrim fleeing from the City of Destruction in such passages, for Spinoza is no dweller in the 'village named Morality' with Mr. Worldly Wiseman who 'savoureth only the Doctrine of this world'—he seeks 'the strait gate that leadeth unto life'; so that those who have interpreted

[1] §§ 1, 7.

his philosophy, with its denial of anthropomorphic personality to God, of indeterminacy to human action, of contingency to eternal Nature, as involving the end of all morality, are far indeed from a true estimate of his purposes. Whether they are equally far from a true estimate of his success in carrying out his purposes, is, of course, another question, but one which it is possible, as we shall see, to answer in the affirmative. So also, those many who have styled him 'atheist' (with Hegel who preferred to regard him as an 'acosmist') are guilty not only of mere paradox (for his doctrine is nothing if not theocentric and cosmological) but of a failure to take due account of his fundamental interest in human salvation by the cultivation of the 'knowledge and love of God'. True philosophy must be a doctrine of both God and the world, and of their relations: of divine agency and of the world's emanation and salvation. Spinoza's metaphysical theory fulfils this requirement as amply, and as adequately, as any that has been thought out: for it is a theory of salvation founded upon a theory of reality. Human wellbeing can only be understood in the light of a knowledge of human nature and of the world in which man is born, struggles, and is improved or degraded in a brief duration; and these again in the light of a knowledge of durational man and universe as related to a reality and a source that is eternal. Thus *Part I* of the *Ethics* is devoted to an account of the divine nature and the eternal universe which is its actuality—the exhaustively determinate expression of its infinite indeterminate potency; *Part II* to the nature of man as typical finite creature, framed on the analogy of his source but subject to the privations of self-reference by which his eternity is degraded to durational form, and his action to *conatus* in part characterized by 'passion' and in part by 'exertion', by which he falls into error and vice, or seeks the way of truth and virtue. *Part III* expounds the natures of these durational dispositions as a preparation for the accounts given in *Parts IV* and *V* of the ways of perdition and salvation, of the nature of the man who supposes that he is free in so far as he is governed by passion, and of the man who is truly free in so far as he eradicates the passions by the cultivation of 'exertions', and finally of the nature of the 'blessedness' by which such a life may be crowned and transformed, its durationality transcended, and its eternal creation realized. The division of topics is, of course, not absolute, for the principles of human salvation themselves enlighten us in no small measure about the natures of 'man, and God, and things', and their relations. This is but an example of the unity of the doctrine which must qualify its linear exposition: the *Parts* cannot be separated without risk of obscurity. And just as the ontological and 'soteriological' doctrines cannot be divorced, so neither can these be understood apart from the epistemological (nor this apart from those). None will seriously dispute the broad validity of Locke's contention that critical appraisement of the 'instrument' of knowledge—the theory of the nature and limits of the cognitive power of the human mind—must precede the theory of the nature and reality of its objects; yet equally it must be asserted that theory of knowledge cannot get very far in the absence of a doctrine of the metaphysical status of the human knower, and of the ontological relations of the knower and the known. God's knowledge of the world is not likely to be identical in form and substance with that of even the wisest of men, just as man's knowledge of it must differ from that of an insect—and not merely in range. For insect and man are parts of the world differing not merely in range, but in potency, and God is in no sense a part of it, but the potency that it actualizes. As soon, therefore, as we seek to pass from the study of specifically *human* knowledge to a doctrine of knowledge *as such*, knowledge of man's epistemological specificity is required, and we must make reference to ontological principles. For apart from this reference we shall be liable, nay, almost certain, to fall into the error, either of supposing that human knowledge is a mere limited range of knowledge in general (the peculiar fallacy of theories of 'natural realism'), or of mistaking what is a mere eccentricity and defect arising from the special status and faculty of man, for the essence and norm of knowledge as such. And this latter error is the essential presupposition of the truncated empiricism to which I have referred, which takes what is merely objectively 'given' in human experience (or given as object for human experience) as the foundation and verificatory norm of knowledge, instead of the 'blind spots' of human understanding.

Sophistries such as these are results of the attempt to elaborate a theory of knowledge without due recourse to metaphysical enlightenment concerning the status and limitations of the human nature from the cognitive activities of which the conception of knowledge is primarily taken. Yet how can this enlightenment be attained in the absence of a satisfactory theory of knowledge? Must not the metaphysics remain in doubt while the epistemology remains incomplete, just as much as the epistemology remains dubious in the absence of the metaphysics? The reply is that the distinction is over-emphasized: we are accustomed to distinguish sharply between 'knowing' and 'being', and the distinction is *epistemically* important; yet 'knowing' is a form of being— the form enjoyed by 'minds' (which are not ghostly 'things' but knowing *agents*). Thus epistemology is essentially the metaphysics of mind, so that the question of philosophical priority lapses; and Spinoza's decision to begin, in the *Ethics*,[1] with a general metaphysical doctrine becomes intelligible, since it is not, as Descartes supposed, from the abstract '*cogito*' that philosophical analysis must proceed, but from the concrete psychophysical '*conor*', by the emendation of which the conception of 'perfect being', or 'agency' is elaborated. And it is from this that the synthetic exposition of the *Ethics* proceeds.

Finally I must here draw the attention of the unwary modern beginner, however briefly, to two connected topics, without a due understanding of which the philosophy of Spinoza must remain wholly obscure, or suffer radical misinterpretation, viz. the conception of 'action', and the distinction which must be drawn between a 'being in itself' (i.e. its real nature) and the objective rendering of the being 'for another' (e.g. as perceived).

The conception of 'action' has well-nigh disappeared from philosophical currency under the influence of a truncated empiricism—being taken to be the exertion of 'effort', which again has been confused with the experienced 'sense of effort' which is easily identified with certain organic sensations, and thus as involving no real *power*. Rightly understood, however, by 'action' is meant the *actualization of potency*. It is thus bipolar, so that there is no 'actuality' that does not stem from 'potency', and no 'potency' that is not actualized. Though *prima facie* this prin-

---

[1] It is noteworthy that the *Tractatus de Intellectus Emendatione*, which is primarily concerned with knowledge and philosophical method, remained unfinished, though doubtless the original intention was to proceed to a general metaphysical conclusion. Having got so far, it would seem, Spinoza saw that the work was unduly cramped by the limitations imposed by the restriction of the basis of his inquiry to the metaphysics of mind. Though valid so far as it went (and thus worth preserving), the more radical scheme of the *Ethics* provided a more liberal and satisfactory field of investigation.

ciple seems to render *durational* action (which Spinoza calls *conatus* or endeavour) paradoxical, since here we seem to be *able* to do what in fact we do not *do*, i.e. to possess a potency not actualized, the paradox arises from the failure to distinguish between the *possession* of potency and its *availability*. A perfect primordial being possesses all potency in eternal act; but an imperfect and privative being possesses only the potency that it actualizes, though, as privative, potency is durationally available to it that is not *by it* durationally actualized. The problems raised by this situation are central in the philosophy of Spinoza.

The second topic is equally vital, for the conception of 'being' is too readily confused with that of 'objective thing'. But objective things are appearances (or it would be truer to say 'occultations') of agents, and it is by their agency alone that such 'presentations' are certified as authentic beings. To 'be' is to 'act', and real beings, i.e. agents, appear as objective things only for the perception of *other* beings, not for their own apprehension. Take, for example, the 'seeing eye': as *seen by another* it is an organic objective thing of a certain shape and structure, with neural and cerebral connexions, so that its 'seeing' becomes a miracle that has defied, and must defy, objective elucidation. But as apprehended by itself it is no such particular objective thing compresent with others, and its 'seeing' is its essential characteristic. Nor is this a mere accident of situation: no seeing eye can see itself as an objective thing (save in a mirror by way of image, with respect to which the seeing eye is *another*). Thus the seeing eye as it is in itself is not the objective thing seen by another, but its own being-in-act. True, it may be supposed to make objective appearance as visive transparency or empty visual field in which presentations appear as 'blind spots' or occultations of its transparency; yet even this objective appearance must be discounted since an *empty* visual field cannot be a 'field'.

In general, then, the reality of a being is its agency, and not its objective thinghood—save in so far as its objectivity involves its agency under *partial* occultation. In qualitied objective things we apprehend agents *'per speculum in aenigmate'*.[1]

---

[1] These topics are more fully discussed and elaborated in my articles: 'On Things in Themselves' (*Philosophy*, xiv, pp. 155–79); 'Knowledge, Reality, and Objectivity' (*Mind*, N.S., xlix, pp. 170–88, 303–32); and 'On a Reputed Equivoque in the Philosophy of Spinoza' (*Review of Metaphysics*, iii, pp. 189–212).

THE DOCTRINE OF BEING

CHAPTER I

'CAUSE OF ITSELF'

I. CAUSATION AS ACTION

The conception of causation is fundamental in the philosophy of Spinoza; but it is causation conceived as action, and not as the mere regular sequence of inactive events. For by 'action' here is meant not change of motion or rest, of content or quality, among spatio-temporal objects, nor of mode or content among mental ideas; on the contrary, mere uniform temporal change is essentially the ideal limit of the privation of action. This at the least was established by Hume. By 'action' is signified the distinction in unity of 'potency' and its 'actuality'. For to say that something is 'actual' is to imply that it is the determinate actuality of some potency-in-act. Agency involves both a power of act*ing* and the expression of that power in something enact*ed*, a doing and a deed, and in action *par excellence* that which is enacted is the exhaustive expression of the potency, without inhibition or frustration, by which agency may otherwise be reduced to durational effort more or less effective. Action is thus originally and essentially eternal, and becomes durational only by limitation and modification. Mere uniform temporal sequence can be styled 'causality' only by way of paradox—*lucus a non lucendo*.

Spinoza's philosophical intention, therefore, is to derive all things from a primordial infinite power or indeterminate potency self-actualized in an infinite and exhaustively determinate eternal universe; and it is thus that he conceives that 'infinite beings follow in infinite ways from the divine nature',[1] i.e. from the self-actualizing creative potency-in-act. The further derivation of the durational world of common experience and science, composed of things that in their order and status are imperfectly active, or conative, thus becomes an essential problem, the solution of which constitutes the chief value of Spinoza's theory—affording

[1] *Eth. I, xvi.*

as it does the clue to that reversal of human privation that constitutes the essential character of morality.

It follows that all interpretations of the doctrine of Spinoza that
fail to take due note of its *activism*, and interpret causation in
terms of the confessedly impotent categories of positivistic theory
are thereby hamstrung from the start, and can only proceed to
further and more mischievous misunderstandings which seem to
involve him in fallacies so futile and obvious as to lie beyond the
possible stupidity of the merest tiro.

Part I of the *Ethics* is chiefly devoted to the clarification of the
principles governing the nature and existence of the eternal self-
actualizing potency, and to the deduction of the formal characteristics of this primordial agent. The essential nature of this
being is laid down in the first definition: 'By *cause of itself* I
understand that the essence of which involves existence.' Such a
being is wholly independent of the operation or existence of what
is other than itself, and is thus real *sans phrase*. That alone is
primordially real that realizes itself as potency-in-act, subject to
no alien contingency.

This primordial being is thus at once both cause and effect, and
critics unable to divest themselves of the common notion of
'cause' have often poured scorn upon the conception. Martineau,[1]
for example, claims that in the phrase *causa sui* the *causa* cancels
the *sui*, and the *sui* cancels the *causa*, and Pollock that the definition 'leaves causation wholly out of account' and 'implies that the
use of the word cause in this sense is really inappropriate'.[2]
Whether the common use of the term 'cause' as implying temporal production or conditioning is in any degree defensible, and
if so how, and in what degree, need not now be canvassed; suffice
it to emphasize once more that it is anachronistic as attributed to
Spinoza. For him causation is the actualization of potency, not
the mere sequence of passive 'events', or even the relation of 'sign'
and 'thing signified', but rather what Berkeley distinguished as
'real causality', involving real power to generate or produce.
Essentially it is not that the cause *has* the power, but that it *is*
the power, and if that power is absolute its actuality (or effect) is,
with it, self-existent.

The primordial Real, then, is the duality in unity of cause or

[1] *A Study of Spinoza*, pp. 117–19, 224–5.
[2] *Spinoza, His Life and Philosophy* (2nd ed.), p. 149.

potency and effect or actuality. Spinoza has several ways of expressing this ultimate nature: as a distinction in identity of (1) 'Substance' and 'mode'; (2) 'Creator' and 'creature'; (3) *'Natura naturans'* and *'Natura naturata'*; (4) 'Essence' and 'expression'. Let us briefly examine these variant modes of expression *seriatim*.

1. *Substance and Mode*

Formal definitions of these terms are given at the beginning of *Part I* of the *Ethics*, and there is therefore no valid excuse to be offered by those who carelessly substitute other uses of them derived from alien sources. Substance does not stand for 'matter' either in its commonsense or its Lockian interpretation. It is not a supposed underlying somewhat in which qualities inhere, but 'that which is in itself and is conceived through itself: that is, that the conception of which does not require the conception of anything other from which it must be formed'.[1] It is self-existent and self-manifest being, self-actualizing and self-certifying being or potency-in-act. The definition of Mode of Substance at once contrasts it with Substance while maintaining their asymmetrical relation: 'By Mode I understand the *affectiones* of Substance, or that which is in another, through which also it is conceived.'[2] Here the interpretation to be placed on the term *'affectio'*, and what it means to be 'in another', and to be conceived 'through another' must be considered.

'In another' is evidently used by way of contrast with the 'in itself' of the definition of substance. Whereas substance is self-existent and self-manifest, what is modal depends for its existence on what transcends, or lies beyond, its own proper nature, and can be conceived only as so related. But this does not mean (as has too often been supposed), at least not primarily and essentially, dependence on extrinsic co-ordinate modes (e.g. on things spatio-temporally other) as things are supposed to depend on their 'natural causes'—a man on his parents, or a tree on the soil and atmosphere, for existence or sustenance. The mode's original 'other' is substance itself as the potency-in-act of which the mode is the actual being thence derived. It is in this sense that Spinoza speaks of certain 'immediate' and 'mediate' infinite and eternal modes of substance[3] (e.g. 'infinite intellect', eternal 'motion and

---

[1] *Eth. I, Def. iii.*   [2] *Eth. I, Def. v.*   [3] *Eth. I, xxi; xxii.* Cf. also *Ep. lxiv.*

rest', and the idea and 'make of the whole universe'), which are the primordial and generically perfect actualizations of divine potency; and here there can be no dependence on extrinsic co-ordinate modes. With the finite modes this dependence on substance entails a *derived* dependence on other finite modes, however, and these function as the *proximate* others of the finite mode under consideration. It is this derived dependence that remains in evidence in the spatio-temporal order which, as we shall see, privatively expresses the eternal order of actualities.

Originally, then, a mode is 'in another' because it is a mode *of substance* which, because the relation of mode and substance is asymmetrical, is for it an 'other'. Yet substance and mode are not symmetrically and mutually other, for the mode is the actuality of the potency-in-act which is substance: it is an *affectio* of substance. But this, again, does not mean that substance is 'affected', or acted upon, by something other than itself, but that it takes a nature by way of self-expression. The meaning lies nearer to our use of the term 'affect' when we say that a man 'affects the aristocrat' than when we say that he is 'affected by the climate'— though there is, of course, no suggestion of pretence: substance actualizes and manifests itself in the mode—it is the active cause, and the mode its enacted effect. Self-actualizing and self-manifesting substance is thus essentially real and intelligible as 'cause of itself', i.e. as creating its own actuality, exhaustively and eternally. The primordial Real is substance as infinite indeterminate potency eternally actualized as exhaustively determinate mode, and is thus self-existent, self-manifest, *causa sui*.

Finally, it is of first importance to remember that just as the 'substance' of Spinoza must not be confused with the 'substances' of other philosophies or of common sense, so also his 'mode' must not be identified with the individual things of temporal human experience. Many, if not most, expositors and critics of Spinoza have suffered shipwreck on this rock. The sense and manner in which such things are 'modes' will, I hope, become clear as we proceed; but here, and in all strictness universally, 'mode' must be taken *au pied de la lettre* of the formal definition: as contrasted with, yet essentially related to, substance. Modes derive their existence from the creative action that is substance; substance realizes itself in the creation of modes, for there is no action without deed. Its existence is necessary by reason of its essence as free action creatively enacting its own expression. For it 'essence' and 'existence', though distinct, are identical.

2. *Creator and Creature*

Substance as cause is thus absolutely free action or creation: it is not a 'thing' but self-realizing and self-manifesting *agency*. Modes as effects of that agency are created beings actualizing the potency of their cause. The notion, sometimes entertained, that Spinoza's substance is a *totum* of which its modes are the parts is too jejune to merit refutation. But again, in using the terms 'creator' and 'creature', with their long association with theology, popular and otherwise (though I do not suppose that theologians of intellectual merit are likely to fall into these errors), we must not be led to think of the modes or created beings as precipitated 'out of nothing' to constitute a world *existentially* divorced from its creator (though deriving its essence from the exercise of his will). We are concerned, not with magic, but with metaphysics. Creative substance did not precede the created modal world in time, and produce it by a dated *fiat* of its ungrounded 'will'. The otherness of the creator is not existential, for the creator exists only as creating. Creation is eternal, and no temporal being is fully 'created'. The emergence of time, and its relation to eternity belong to a later stage of our analysis.

It was, perhaps, because of the danger of misinterpretation by minds ill-trained in theology that Spinoza almost entirely excluded from the *Ethics* this terminology which he had not hesitated to adopt and define in his earlier works, the *Cogitata Metaphysica* and the *Short Treatise*. But I do not think that this indicates any radical change in his view. Nor is the exclusion complete.[1]

I have said that creation is an eternal action, and that therefore created things are eternal. This implies that durational beings are not, as such, 'creatures' in the full sense. It will be well, therefore, to postpone further discussion of this mode of expression until the mode of egression of such beings comes to be considered.

[1] Cf. *Eth. I, Append.*

3. 'Natura naturans' *and* 'Natura naturata'

Spinoza also expounds the primordial nature of the Real by the use of the medieval conceptions thus expressed. The significance of the terms '*Natura naturans*' and '*Natura naturata*' may be traced as far back as the great Greek philosophers: but here it may suffice to say that beginning at least with Plato the distinction makes inchoate appearance in the Aristotelian discrimination of the 'unmoved mover' and 'that which is moved'. This was utilized by Augustine, and developed by Scotus Eriugena into a distinction and identification of God and the world. 'Nature' as creative potency-in-act is God—Nature as creating a nature for itself: Nature 'naturing itself'; Nature regarded as a determinate totality of determinate being—as having received a nature—is the world or Nature 'natured'. This mode of expression and thought was further developed by the Arabian philosopher Averroës, and it reappeared in the thought of the Renaissance philosopher-poet Giordano Bruno. Whether it reached Spinoza from this source, or from earlier or intermediate sources, Jewish or otherwise, we have no certain knowledge. Spinoza expressly defines his use of the terms in *Ethices I, xxix, Sch.*: 'By *Natura naturans* we must understand that which is in itself and is conceived through itself, or those attributes of substance which express eternal and infinite essence, that is, God in so far as he is considered as a free cause. By *Natura naturata* I understand all that follows from the necessity of God's nature, or of any one of God's attributes, that is, all the modes of the attributes of God in so far as they are considered as things which are in God, and which without God can neither be nor be conceived.' This definitely identifies the distinction with that of Substance and Mode as the integral *termini* of creation. Nature, the primordial real, is a unity of agency and deed, and is thus asymmetrically bipolar: as infinite indeterminate potency-in-act it is *Natura naturans*: as *actus*, i.e. the exhaustively determinate actuality, of this potency it is *Natura naturata*. Genetically God is prior to the world; ontologically they are identical as indeterminately infinite and infinitely determinate. It is in this sense that Spinoza speaks of 'God or Nature'—for though in all strictness God is *Natura naturans*, the identity of this with *Natura naturata* validates the phrase. But, of course, *Natura naturata* is not to be identified with the durational world of common experience—the 'common order of nature', which is temporal, multiplex, and divided—it is the eternal 'make of the whole universe', infinite, one, and indivisible, of which the durational world is but a privation. The common objections to the identification of God and Nature thus collapse, since the durational world with its manifold imperfections is not, by Spinoza, regarded as being incorrigibly divine or fully created.

4. *Essence and Expression*

Spinoza sometimes speaks of the primordial causality which is the essential constitution of 'God or Nature' as the 'expression' of its essence in existence.[1] This is, perhaps, a somewhat less happy mode of statement, because we are apt to think of 'expression' under the analogy of the fashioning of something physical—characters, sounds, or artistic and other artificial products—in accordance with ideas or mental conceptions. But Spinoza must not be taken as conceiving creative action on the analogy of such verbal or artistic 'expression' of ideas in another medium. For Substance, *Natura naturans*, or God is not exclusively mental; nor is modal being, *Natura naturata*, or the eternal universe exclusively non-mental. These are not two beings having the same form, or having different forms conventionally associated, in different materials. We have yet to deal with the distinction of the mental and the physical, and their relation, as it is understood by Spinoza, but they are certainly not to be identified with those of creator and creature. Undoubtedly, for Spinoza the eternal extended universe which is the actuality of Substance as 'extension' may be regarded as an 'expression' of Substance as 'thought', but equally the eternal psychical universe which is its actuality as 'thought' may be regarded as an 'expression' of Substance as 'extension'. This does but emphasize the identity of 'extension' and 'thought' as 'attributes' of Substance. Their distinction is intellectual, i.e. with *respect* to intellect; and it is because philosophy is an intellectual discipline that the creative actualization of potency comes to be conceived as 'expression'. Danger, however, lurks in this usage, viz. that of exclusive 'intellectualism' which forgets that intellect, which for man as

[1] In this connexion see F. Kaufmann, 'Spinoza's System as Theory of Expression' (*Philos. and Phenomenol. Research*, 1940, pp. 83–97).

philosopher is basic, is but a modal being—and not the exclusive actuality of Substance.

II. SUBSTANCE AND ATTRIBUTE

We are thus led next to a consideration of the nature of the Attributes of Substance, their interrelation, and status with respect to 'God or Nature'. Spinoza's formal definition of 'Attribute' indicates clearly enough that the term is not to be taken in the vulgar sense of a characteristic or quality related to Substance as, e.g., sobriety is related to Peter, or redness to a rose: 'By attribute I understand that which the intellect perceives of substance as constituting its essence.'[1] The attributes of Substance, then, are the essence of Substance as apprehended, and truly, by intellect: they do not *inhere* in it, but *constitute* its essence. This is further emphasized by Spinoza in *Epistola ix*: 'By substance I mean that which is in itself, and is conceived through itself. *I mean the same by attribute* except that it is called "attribute" with respect to intellect which attributes such and such a nature to substance.'[2] It is equally important, however, not to place an illegitimate emphasis on the relation with intellect as many expositors have done under the influence of idealistic developments from which Spinoza was entirely free. No Kantian or idealistic significance is to be attached to Spinoza's words: intellect does not necessarily condemn itself to phenomenalism by merely imputing the Attributes to Substance that as a 'thing-in-itself' is devoid of them. Nor on the other hand, is the Real limited by intellect whether human or divine. What intellect perceives it perceives truly, for that is the nature of intellect: imagination and its modes are *privations* of intellect. Yet human intellect, circumscribed as it is in its range of objects (though essentially self-transcendent), though it suffers no privation such as to lead it to error, is nevertheless imperfect and, as Spinoza says, differs from infinite intellect 'as the Dog in the heavens differs from the barking animal'.[3] The Attributes of Substance are thus neither qualities or characteristics of Substance nor its phenomenal appearances due to the relativity of human intellect. The Attribute *is* the Substance under the determining scrutiny of intellect. In the letter from which I have already quoted, Spin-

---

[1] *Eth. I, Def. iv.*   [2] My italics.   [3] *Eth. I, xvii, Sch.*

oza offered his correspondent two examples to illustrate the kind of distinction he had in mind: (1) the third patriarch, Israel, was also called Jacob (i.e. supplanter) because he seized his brother's heel; again (2) a plane surface is one that reflects all rays of light without any other change—it is called 'white' in relation to a man observing it. What both examples bring home is evidently the notion of 'respect': what distinguishes an Attribute from Substance is that it is the same but in a different respect; and we know from the definition of 'Attribute' that this respect is respect to *intellect*. Now intellect is not extrinsic to Nature, like a spectator at the games, but is involved in it. Nor is it as such substantial (for substance is indeterminate). It is therefore a mode or actualization of Substance. Thus the respect by which an Attribute is distinguished from Substance is intrinsic—not like that of Jacob to Isaac, or the plane surface to the observer; and the Attribute is Substance with respect to one of its own actualizations. Substance, we have seen, is infinite and eternal potency-in-act, and as such absolutely indeterminate; its actualization consists in its exhaustive determination. But what in itself is absolutely indeterminate must, with respect to its determinate actualizations be a *determining* agency, and thus *reflectively determinate*. As actualizing the determinate its indeterminacy is specified, i.e. intellect as an actual determination of Substance perceives the essence of Substance as a potency-in-act whence flows the specific determinations involved in or essential to intellect. Thus *human* intellect perceives Substance as infinite and eternal *thinking* potency-in-act and as infinite and eternal '*extension*' or physical potency-in-act.

This is the root of the distinction both of the Attributes and of Substance and Attributes. Though Substance in itself is absolutely indeterminate, with respect to its determinate actualizations it is generically determinate—'generically', because as infinite and eternal only the universal properties of finite modes can be unconditionally imputed to Substance. Why, then, it may be asked, does Spinoza single out *intellect* as the referent by which Attributes are distinguished from Substance? The answer is simple enough: because the purpose of philosophy is to make Nature *intelligible*, so that this respect to intellect must be, for it, central.

Further, though *human* intellect thus perceives Substance as

c

thinking and physical potency-in-act, in so far as these potencies are reflectively determinate the nature of Substance in itself cannot be confined to these Attributes. An absolutely indeterminate potency cannot be the source merely of determinate psychical and physical actuality, for thus it would not be indeterminate but psycho-physical potency-in-act. Its absolute indeterminacy necessitates the inference to infinite Attributes; for only the infinitely determinate can exhaustively actualize the absolutely indeterminate.

The *conceived* (and truly conceived) distinctions of the infinite Attributes of Substance is thus with respect to the actualization of one of them, viz. Thought. Substance as such suffers no such distinction, nevertheless these distinctions are valid since from its very nature as potency-in-act Substance exists only as self-actualizing—as producing infinite things 'in infinite ways'. It may be objected that it is paradoxical to say that Substance is both absolutely indeterminate and also 'consists of infinite Attributes'—and indeed it would be so if the nature of Substance provided no 'logical room' for this disparity, if, for example, Substance were a 'thing' and not an *agent*. The apparent contradiction is 'dialectical' or self-resolved in the conception of creative agency.

For philosophy, then, i.e. for intellect, the primordial Real or Substance actively functioning as creator consists of infinite Attributes 'each of which expresses eternal and infinite essence'. This is 'God or Nature'.

CHAPTER II

'GOD OR NATURE'

In the foregoing account of Substance, its Modes, and its Attributes, I have trespassed somewhat beyond the account given by Spinoza himself in the Definitions and first ten Propositions of *Part I* of the *Ethics*. In these he is primarily concerned with the conceptions alone, without reference to their precise application to the primordial and consequent Real. It is only in *Proposition xi* that he turns explicitly to metaphysical assertion, and identifies the Real with 'Substance consisting of infinite Attributes each of which expresses eternal and infinite essence'; and we have to wait until *Proposition xvi* before learning that the Modes of this Substance are 'infinite beings flowing in infinite ways' from the necessity of its nature.

Reality, we have seen, means agency, not mere objective givenness, and in agency we discern potency-in-act and actuality—or, in other words, essence and existence.

I. ESSENCE OR POTENCY-IN-ACT

'God or Nature', Spinoza repeatedly affirms, is 'infinite, one, and indivisible'. It will be convenient to consider these essential properties in the reverse order:

1. *Indivisible*

'Substance absolutely infinite is indivisible':[1] the infinity of the Attributes of Substance does not entail multiplicity of essences. This follows from the nature of an Attribute, which has already been considered. An Attribute is the determin*ing* nature of Substance with respect to some *determinatum* (e.g. intellect) of its absolutely indeterminate potency-in-act. For it is of the nature of creation that absolutely indeterminate potency is actualized in determinate beings of every conceivable kind, and it is with

[1] *Eth. I, xiii.*

respect to these universal kinds that Substance is generically determinate to infinity, i.e. 'consists of infinite Attributes', *each* of which (and not the *aggregate* of which) constitutes the essence of Substance. For to say that its Attributes are infinite *in number* is but to deny that they are numerable. In Substance as such the Attributes are neither one nor many, but infinite—for Substance is absolutely indeterminate, though infinitely determining. It is true that the human intellect, e.g., enumerates the Attributes that fall within its cognizance, viz. Thought and Extension, but as thus imputing duality to the divine essence man's knowledge of that essence, though formally adequate, remains clouded by a determinacy that must be transcended in Substance—hence the insistence on the infinity of the Attributes in spite of human limitations. Not that for man Thought and Extension are wholly unrelated and disjoined: they are united in the epistemic, or subject and object, relation of 'experience' in which alone they are discerned. But it is the limitation of human nature as a mode of Thought and Extension alone that renders them discernible, though undivided and infinite in potency. For man Extension is at once essential to Thought as its primary object, and Thought to the discernment of Extension, the character of each being revealed by contrast with the other. Thus in 'experience' Thought and Extension are at once realized and discerned as *epistemically* indivisible. Yet 'experience', too, has a determinate character which (*pace* the 'Experience-philosophers') disqualifies it for identification with Substance; and the substantial nature of Thought, or of Extension, or of any of the infinite Attributes of Substance, is realized only in the absolute 'unity' of Substance— a unity infinitely more intimate than the epistemic unity of 'experience'. As so united, *substantial* Thought is identical with *substantial* Extension, *substantial* X, etc. For the determinacy of each Attribute in the modal perspective is but the obfuscation of its own implicit negativity qualified by the clarity explicit by its discernment from another with which it is epistemically, or otherwise, united and indivisible. It is thus that the divine intellect, which is the actuality of *substantial* Thought, infinitely transcends the human intellect, which is but the actuality of Thought as an Attribute epistemically united with Extension alone in determinate 'experience'. 'If intellect pertains to the divine nature it cannot, like ours, follow the things which are its objects (as many suppose), nor can it be simultaneous in its nature with them, since God is prior to all things in causality, but on the contrary, the truth and formal essence of things is what it is because as such it exists by way of knowledge in God's intellect. Therefore the intellect of God, in so far as it is conceived as constituting his essence' (i.e. as potency-in-act) 'is in truth the cause of things, both of their essence and of their existence.'[1] But this is not a peculiarity of Thought, for *mutatis mutandis* the same may be asserted of all the Attributes which in Substance are indivisible.[2]

2. *Unique*

God, or Substance consisting of infinite Attributes, is not one among many but beside it no substance can be or be conceived.[3] This follows from the definition of God as 'Substance consisting of infinite Attributes': for thus all Attributes are attributed to it, and substances with the same attribute are not discernible or distinct.[4] Spinoza takes occasion in both *Ethices I, xiv. Cor. ii* and *xv Sch.* to deal with the conventional view (entertained by Descartes) that extended substance is created, and additional to the creative Substance or God, pointing out that the arguments adduced in favour of this arise from the misconstruing of the nature of extended substance. He allows that God is not 'corporeal' in the sense of possessing a 'body' determined in length, breadth and depth. Such a conception of Extension, whether taken to be a substance or an Attribute, is erroneous: all 'bodies' are but its finite modes or actualizations: Extension as such is extensional potency-in-act.[5] But this being so, and all potency being proper to 'God or Nature', Extension, though substantial,

---

[1] *Eth. I, xvii, Sch.*
[2] Here we have confined attention to Substance, or God as *Natura naturans*; but it may be added that no ground for the imputation of divisibility to this can be drawn from the multiplicity inherent in *Natura naturata*, or the finite modes of Substance, to be considered in the next chapter; for even here the multiplicity is fully integral when we consider 'the whole order of nature'. *Natura naturata* as it actualizes *Natura naturans*, is 'infinite, unique, and indivisible'; for each individual part focalizes the whole which is thus immanent in each. *Natura naturata* is not an aggregate of parts but a macrocosm of microcosms to infinity.
[3] *Eth. I, xiv.*
[4] *Eth. I, v.*
[5] The alternative interpretation of Extension as empty three-dimensional space is, of course, equally improper.

can be no substance distinct from the infinite creative Substance.[1]

A word is perhaps required concerning Spinoza's distinction
of 'unity' or 'singleness' as applied to 'God or Nature' and its
'uniqueness'—the former description being regarded by him as
'very improper'. 'A thing can only be said to be one or single in
respect of its existence and not of its essence: for we do not conceive things under numbers until they have been brought under
a common genus. . . . Hence it is clear that nothing can be called
one or single unless some other thing has been conceived which
agrees with it.'[2] Thus, the uniqueness of 'God or Nature' follows
from its indeterminate infinity as essence or potency-in-act which
excludes the possibility of another.

3. *Infinite*

In his *Letter on the Nature of the Infinite*[3] Spinoza distinguishes
between 'infinite by nature or definition', 'limitless', and 'in-
numerable'. Now Substance, the primordial potency-in-act, is by
nature indivisible, and hence its infinity cannot mean limitless
multiplicity of parts. Again, since it is unique its infinity cannot
mean the indefinite remoteness of extrinsic limits, or, indeed, the
mere absence of limits. Its infinity (in spite of the negative suggestion of the term itself) is 'by nature or definition'; and this has
application not only to its nature as 'substance' (for 'every substance is necessarily infinite'),[4] but also to its special nature as
'consisting of infinite Attributes each of which expresses . . . infinite essence'.[5] The Attributes are infinite *in number* only with
respect to the intellect by which they are distinguished. Substance
is infinite as potency-in-act, potency being, as such, by nature
indeterminate, i.e. involving no negation, either intrinsic (for it is
indivisible) or extrinsic (for it is unique). It is only when Substance is conceived as modally actual that the infinity of 'God or
Nature' can be interpreted as limitlessness or innumerability, and
that a 'part' of *Natura naturata* (such as a man) can be regarded

---

[1] It must be admitted that the Cartesian phrase 'extend*ed* Substance' is misleading and, indeed, paradoxical. The comparable phrase, 'think*ing* Substance'
is more correct. And the same applies to the Spinozistic phrases '*res extensa*' and
'*res cogitans*'.

[2] *Ep. l.*   [3] *Ep. xii.*   [4] *Eth. I, viii.*   [5] *Eth. I, xi.*

as '*Deus quatenus finitus est*',[1] and the Attributes which it expresses as numerable, e.g. Thought and Extension. And even so the finiteness of the 'part', and the numerability of the Attributes involved, are not absolute, but must be qualified by essential relation with a complement, and by the limitless numerability of the Attributes, respectively.

Thus, Substance, 'God', or *Natura naturans*, is infinite by nature or definition, and can in no wise be *conceived* as finite (though we may attempt so to *imagine* it). But *Natura naturata*, abstractedly conceived is infinite in virtue of its cause, viz. *Natura naturans*, and can be divided into parts, and viewed as an indefinitely great assemblage of such parts. Yet this is to conceive it as merely 'given', as 'actual' but not 'enacted', after the fashion of the empiricists. For *Natura naturata* is only properly conceived as eternally flowing from the primordial potency-in-act; and as so conceived it, too, is infinite by nature or definition. And so again, its finite 'parts' are not mere *sectors* of the 'whole', but exist only in relation with their complement, and thus as 'microcosms' or 'finite-infinites'. This is a topic to which we must presently return.

II. EXISTENCE OR ACTUALITY

'God or Nature' exists or is actual as *Natura naturata* exhaustively and determinately realizing the infinite, indeterminate potency-in-act that is *Natura naturans*. This self-actualization is neither a mere possibility, nor is it contingent, but necessary. Thus the actual world is the only possible world.[2]

1. *Possibility, Contingency, and Necessity*

Spinoza had had conversations with Leibniz, and it is conceivable and perhaps even probable that *Ethices I, xxxiii* was directly aimed at the Leibnizian conception of infinite possible worlds in the mind of God, from which he chose the best for creation. The

---

[1] Cf. *Eth. II, ix; xi, Cor.* As difficulties have been raised by some commentators concerning this doctrine of the relation of man and God (cf. H. Barker 'Notes on the Second Part of Spinoza's *Ethics*', *Mind*, N.S., xlvii, pp. 437 *et passim*) it may be well to say here that Spinoza does not equate the human mind as durationally extant with '*Deus quatenus humanae mentis essentiam constituit*', but only as thinking adequately.

[2] *Eth. I, xxxiii.*

idea is anthropomorphic, interpreting creation as a sort of artistic production *ex nihilo*. It fails by reason of the paradoxical nature of the being which must be imputed to the uncreated possible worlds which are at once 'ideally' actual and also merely possible. For nothing can be said to be *merely* possible if 'possible' is distinguished from 'contingent', that being contingent that is known to issue from a cause the existence of which remains in doubt.[1] Now all that exists or is actual is the actuality of potency-in-act original or derived, and it is thus that actual existence is necessary though not extrinsically compelled. Necessity, rightly understood, is true freedom or potency-in-act. This is not to deny that *durational* things are authentically contingent in so far as the occurrence of durational causes cannot be certainly foretold by durational minds. But, as we shall see, durational things are privations of eternal beings, and their contingency is concomitant with their privativity. As referred to this or that finite 'part' of *Natura naturata* they may be authentically contingent, but as referred to God they are certainly necessary.

Now, when we consider 'God or Nature' as *causa sui* no such distinction of certain necessity and authentic contingency can be entertained, much less any notion of its being merely possible; for *Natura naturata* is the very exhaustively determinate actuality of the infinite indeterminate primordial potency-in-act that is *Natura naturans*. Because that potency is infinite, unique and indivisible, its actuality is perfect and necessary. For a 'potency' not 'in-act' is no potency at all.

2. *Proofs of the Existence of God*

Those who thus far have followed the development of Spinoza's doctrine will notice with no surprise that he concludes the real existence of God in a laconic inference occupying but three lines of the text: 'If it be denied, conceive that God does not exist.

---

[1] It should not be necessary to point out that *mere possibility* must be distinguished from *potentiality* (though even philosophers of high repute have sometimes failed to discern them, and rejected the one on the ground of the vacuity of the other). A block of marble 'has the possibility' of becoming an Apollo (or many another statue), but not the potentiality, even in the sense in which an acorn 'has the potentiality' of becoming an oak tree (and no other)—though even here the potency is not wholly intrinsic or immanent (as with the *causa sui* or an eternal *creatum*).

Then his essence does not involve existence; which is absurd.'[1]
That he also deigns to add two or three other proofs, *a priori* or
a posteriori in form, implies no recognition of dissatisfaction with
this essential proof, which indeed is involved in all of them as
conditio sine qua non.

The first additional proof proceeds from the principle that
what exists or is actual is so by reason of a cause or potency-in-
act, and what does not exist fails to exist by reason of the opposition of some cause or potency-in-act. This cause of existence or
non-existence must lie either in the nature of the thing itself or
beyond it: in its nature when it is necessary or impossible;
beyond it when it is contingent. That for which there is nothing,
intrinsic or extrinsic, that can prevent existence, exists necessarily (the main proof); thus 'God or Nature', which is 'absol-
lutely infinite and consummately perfect' so exists.

The second additional proof is *a posteriori* in form, proceeding
from the existence of 'ourselves'. This existence implies a 'power
to exist' possessed by such finite beings; and if God did not exist
the power of these beings to exist would exceed that of a being
absolutely infinite; which is absurd. Thus either nothing exists
or God exists necessarily.

But as he says in the *Scholium* that follows: 'In this last demon-
stration I wished to prove the existence of God *a posteriori*, not
because it does not follow *a priori* from the same premisses, but
in order that the proof might be more easily understood.' He then
gives the *a priori* form of this *a posteriori* proof (forming a third
additional proof): To be able to exist is a potency, and it follows
that the greater the potency the greater the ability to exist. Now
'God or Nature' is defined as absolutely infinite in potency, and
therefore exists necessarily. Here the point is, of course, that
power to exist is not an extrinsic power imputed to God but God's
very essence from which existence or actuality flows.

It needs little acuity of perception to recognize the equivalence
or dependence of all these proofs upon the same principle, viz.
that expressed in the main proof, commonly called the 'ontological proof'. I say 'equivalence with' or 'dependence upon', for
a distinction may be drawn according as the proofs are, in Cartesian phrase, 'analytic' or 'synthetic' in method. The 'ontological proof' is, of course, as such 'synthetic', proceeding from

[1] *Eth. I, xi.*

essence to existence, from potency-in-act to actuality; the additional proofs, especially the *a posteriori* one, involve 'analytic' procedure from existences, taken to be authentic, by the emendation of essences to an actuality certified by perfect essence or potency-in-act. But the emendation of imperfect essences taken as authentically actual itself proceeds only in the light of the 'ontological principle' of the dependence of actuality or existence upon potency or essence.

This 'analytic' form of proof, though allied with that which Kant oddly styled the 'cosmological proof', and rejected, must carefully be distinguished from it. It does not argue from existences 'contingent' in the sense of caused wholly extrinsically, and thus fortuitous, to a being necessarily existent as the ground of such being taken as authentic or 'given'. To be wholly dependent on extrinsic potency is to be nothing at all; every authentic existent must in part at least actualize its own potency-in-act, and the argument runs that dependence on extrinsic potency is a measure of finiteness and imperfection not suffered by 'God or Nature'. Nor can it be validly supposed that the authentic existence of anything (which the proof assumes as starting point) can be merely hypothetical—depending on an infinite regression of causes, all hypothetical. It is not (as Spinoza points out in *Epistola xii*) that such a regression is impossible, but that the authentic existence of any part of the series requires a passage beyond hypothesis, i.e. to a being dependent on no extrinsic cause, the existence of which actualizes its own intrinsic potency-in-act. If anything exists, *a fortiori* self-dependent being exists.

The 'ontological proof', properly so called, is the 'synthetic' form of the argument, which moves, not from imperfect to perfect being, but from perfect essence to necessary existence, from infinite indeterminate potency-in-act to exhaustively determinate actuality or existence. For the divine essence is not the mere conception of God to which existence must be superadded, but the infinite potency-in-act which necessarily actualizes itself.

The 'ontological proof' has often been subjected to destructive criticism—sometimes validly, when it has been advanced in eccentric form. Kant is often said to have given it its final *quietus* in his celebrated figure of the 'hundred thalers'. Real existence, he argued, is not a 'predicate' which by mere predication precipitates a concept into the real world. To think of a hundred thalers as existing is not the same as to add them to one's bank balance. Similarly, we can gain no assurance of the real existence of God from merely thinking of him as existing. What is truly astonishing is that a thinker of Kant's unquestionable acuity and authority should have supposed that such a refutation has any impact on the genuine ontological proof. Even Descartes had realized that the mere thought of existence is no ground for its certain attribution, and that the nerve of the argument lies in the principle that 'in the concept or idea of everything that is clearly and distinctly conceived' existence is 'contained', existence possible or necessary, such a concept or idea being 'true'.[1] And Hegel ridiculed the suggestion that God can rightly be conceived as in this matter comparable with 'every wretched form of existence'.[2] What is at the root of the general dissatisfaction with the ontological proof is a false opinion about the nature ascribable to God, and derivatively about the natures of all authentic existents, viz. that 'reality' means mere objective 'givenness' and not *agency*—existence being related to essence as actuality to potency-in-act. The actuality of Kant's hundred thalers stems from extrinsic potency-in-act, whereas that of God from infinite intrinsic potency in-act. Thus the one is contingent on the actuality of that from which it stems, the other is necessary.

III. ESSENCE AND EXISTENCE

Finally, the relations and distinction of essence and existence in 'God or Nature', i.e. of the infinite indeterminate primordial potency-in-act and its infinitely determinate enactment or actuality, serve to determine Spinoza's account of the divine causality as *free* and as *immanent*, and being both free and immanent, as *eternal*. With 'God or Nature' essence and existence are at once identical and distinct as the indeterminate is identical with and distinct from its exhaustive determinations—a complex relation which is generally expressed by Spinoza in the form: 'The essence of God *involves* existence.'

[1] Cf. *Meditationes, Resp. ad Obj. I.*
[2] *Lectures on the Philosophy of Religion* (trans. Spiers and Sanderson), iii, 363.

1. *Identical: Causality and Freedom*

Because the actuality of the divine potency-in-act is its exhaustively determinate expression, it follows that the divine action or causality is self-originated and in accordance with its own laws, uncompelled and uninhibited. 'God alone is a free cause; for God alone exists and acts from the necessity alone of his own nature.'[1] The unique necessity of his creative action is identical with perfect or absolute freedom, for God necessarily creates all that his infinite potency involves. To suppose that God would be more free if he could 'bring it about that those things that follow from his nature should not be' is to suppose that he would be more perfect if he lacked a potency which is his (for a potency not 'in-act' is no potency)—a palpable absurdity. To suppose, again, that God's 'freedom' is elective is to deny his omni-potency. For election entails inhibition of potency, i.e. its negation. For the divine nature altogether transcends that of durational man who can be conceived as perfecting himself by the exercise of elective freedom, thus offsetting the privation concomitant with durationality. With 'God or Nature', not to create all within his power is not to increase, but to limit, perfection.

2. *Distinct: Causality and Immanence*

Again, because the divine actuality, i.e. all the beings created by the divine potency-in-act, is exhaustively determinate while that potency is absolutely indeterminate, it follows that the distinction of creator and creature must be so maintained as to define their relation as *causal*, yet without recession from the identity of power and act. It is thus that the causality of God must be conceived as *immanent* in all actual beings, and not as transeunt or agency terminating in some alien actuality.[2] Divine causality is causality *par excellence*, and all relations that can in any sense or degree be called 'causal' are framed on its analogy. Causality, according to Spinoza, is not a temporal relation, not such as was destructively analysed by Hume and defended by Kant; it consists not in regularity of temporal sequence but in agency immanent in deed. Empirical transeunt causes, in so far as they are

---

[1] *Eth. I, xvii, Cor. ii.*   [2] *Eth. I, xviii.*

authentic, possess something of this real power, though in a privative and derivative form (a point obscurely expounded even by
Kant); but so far as they are transeunt, so that the effect lies beyond the cause, they are evidently devoid of it. The causality of
God suffers no such defect, and his effects, therefore, are integral
with their cause, which is immanent in them. The two poles of
divine creation, *Natura naturans* and *Natura naturata* are indiscerptible, though not co-ordinate, transeunt, or alternative. *Natura
naturata* is dependent upon and subordinate to *Natura naturans*,
which in turn necessarily actualizes itself as *Natura naturata*.

3. *Eternal*

It follows that 'God or Nature' is eternal.[1] Here we must recall
the definition of 'eternity': it is 'existence itself in so far as it is
conceived as following necessarily from the essence of the thing'[2]
—and Spinoza adds the *Explanation* that 'it cannot be explicated
by duration or time, not even if this be conceived as without beginning or end'. Eternity is not duration 'from eternity' 'to eternity' (though in time it is *always* available). But neither is it
'timelessness', but a form of *existence* transcending duration. He
speaks of it as an 'infinite existence',[3] as distinct from duration
which is a form of existence conceived as indefinite continuance
in actual being.[4] Durational existence involves *conatus* operative against opposing powers;[5] eternal existence is action, free
and creative. For action *par excellence* is freedom, but as qualified
by opposing agency is constricted to endeavour. And this is the
field of elective freedom, but eternity of free necessity. Thus the
existence of 'God or Nature' is no struggling continuance through
time, but an eternal 'enjoyment'. Nor can the nature of this
'infinite existence' be apprehended on any analogy of transition in time, though we make some rough approach to apprehension in the contemplation of our naïve experience of 'acting'
that defines what we appropriately call the 'specious present' (for
the 'present' is the 'moment' of action), and inadequately
express as the permeation of the future by the past within a small
tract of time. Yet this is but a 'rough approach' because our
'action' remains durational endeavour rather than creativity or

[1] *Eth. I, xix.*   [2] *Eth. I, Def. viii.*   [3] *Cog. Met., II, i.*
[4] *Eth. II, Def. v.*   [5] See below, Ch. IV.

free necessity. It is in pure thought alone that we have experience of eternity, in rational intellection or in intellectual intuition; for 'demonstrations are the eyes of the mind by which it sees and observes things'[1]—and by 'demonstrations', as we shall see in due course, Spinoza does not mean timeless formal syllogisms, but the real self-generation of concepts. Indeed, in intellectual intuition alone, because it is love rather than perception of objects, community rather than contemplation, is eternal life 'enjoyed'; rational intellection apprehends things only 'sub quadam specie aeternitatis'. The existence of 'God or Nature' is the eternal enjoyment of creativity, uncompelled and uninhibited.

[1] *Eth. V, xxiii, Sch.*

CHAPTER III

THE MODES OF SUBSTANCE

The modal actuality of the divine potency-in-act, or Substance, as it flows thence is infinite and eternal, and like it unique and indivisible. But unlike it, it is exhaustively determinate: 'From the necessity of the divine nature there must follow infinite beings in infinite ways'[1]—yet all so as to form a unique and indivisible universe. It follows that *Natura naturata* is itself eternal, and contains nothing that is not eternal. For the divine potency-in-act is uninhibited and can be actualized in no durational being, whether durational as a whole or durational in its parts. Nor can an eternal whole be conceived as the integration of durational parts.

Spinoza distinguishes modes which are infinite, constituting the whole of nature, and modes which are finite parts of nature; and since these raise difficulties of different kinds we shall do well to give them separate consideration.

I. 'INFINITE AND ETERNAL MODES'

Natura naturata is evidently an infinite and eternal mode of Substance or *Natura naturans* of which it is the exhaustive actuality; but a more precise delineation requires consideration of the nature of Substance as 'consisting of infinite Attributes'—for though these are only intellectually discerptible, philosophy in which we are engaged is an intellectual discipline. It is in the light of the distinctions of the Attributes that Spinoza draws a further distinction between 'immediate' and 'mediate' infinite and eternal modes of Substance. For when we consider Substance as *thinking* potency-in-act (i.e. the Attribute of Thought), its *immediate* actuality is that which Thought as such accomplishes, viz. understanding (*intellectus*); and it is as such that understanding is an infinite and eternal mode of Substance and finds expression as the exhaustive idea of thinking Nature (*infinita idea Dei*), which thus becomes the *mediate* infinite and

[1] *Eth. I, xvi.*

eternal mode of Substance *qua* Thought. So again, when we consider Substance as *extensional* potency-in-act (i.e. the Attribute
of Extension), its *immediate* actuality is the 'motion and rest'[1]
inherent in the act of 'extending'; and it is as such that 'motion
and rest' is an infinite and eternal mode of Substance and finds
expression in the 'fashion or make of the whole universe' (*facies
totius universi*),[2] which thus becomes the *mediate* infinite and
eternal mode of Substance *qua* Extension.

II. DETERMINATION AND INDIVIDUATION

Next, we must turn to the nature and status of the finite modes
of Substance which, as I have said, must be distinguished from
finite durational beings, empirical or scientific—being necessarily eternal as pertaining to the actuality of Substance. Potency
qua potency is indeterminate; its actuality *qua* actuality is determinate; potency-in-act is determination. It follows that an infinite potency is actualized as infinitely determinate, involving
every kind and range of existence—yet remaining unique and
indivisible.

---

[1] 'Motion and rest' as the immediate actuality of extensional potency-in-act is
thus not to be identified, or confused, with mere spatio-temporal passage and
stillness. But neither is the phrase a portmanteau expression for motion recognized as being essentially relative to conventional axes, and thus only electively
determinate. Descartes had defined the 'proper motion' of a body as its 'transference from the vicinity of contiguous bodies taken to be at rest' (*Principles of
Philosophy, II, Art. 24–6*) and claimed that this is neither spatially absolute nor
relative merely to conventional axes, but 'a mode of the mobile body'—its mode
(let us say) of 'attachment' to whatsoever body may be contiguous with it: its
intrinsic restlessness. Similarly, its 'proper rest' must be its quiescence with
respect to whatsoever body may be contiguous with it; its intrinsic inertia. A
body's 'proper motion and rest' remains unchanged through all vicissitudes,
while the body itself remains identical, though its speed and direction of motion
are subject to variation under impact. It is but a short step from this account to
the view of 'motion and rest' as modes of physical agency rather than passive
spatio-temporal transference and stillness, absolute or conventional. And if this
conception is delimited, 'motion and rest' as the immediate infinite and eternal
mode of Substance *qua* Extension must be conceived as the actuality of extensional potency-in-act inseparably issuing therefrom.

[2] This phrase, naïvely translated as 'the *face* of the whole universe' has
usually been taken as referring to the spatio-temporal world of experience, the
'visible universe', i.e. what Spinoza calls 'the common order of nature'. This is
certainly an error, and the translation of '*facies*' by 'fashion or make' (*facio*) is to
be recommended. Extensional *Natura naturata* is not imaginationally quantita-
tive and temporal, but infinite and eternal. The phrase is used in *Ep. liv.*

We have seen already that this is the source of the distinctions of the infinite Attributes of Substance in the reflective modal perspective of 'intellect'. But the infinite determination of actual Nature is not to be limited to the generic distinctions of the Attributes: it is *exhaustively* determinate. 'From the necessity of the divine nature infinite beings must follow in infinite ways, i.e. everything that can be conceived by infinite intellect';[1] or as it is expressed even more vigorously in the *Appendix* to *Part I* of the *Ethics*: To God 'material was not lacking for the creation of everything, from the highest to the very lowest grade of perfection; or, to speak more properly, . . . the laws of his nature were so ample that they sufficed for the production of everything conceivable by infinite intellect'. Not only is 'God or Nature' actual in infinite sorts of existence, cognitive, extensional, 'X-ian', but also in infinite grades or ranges under each generic head, from the infinite immediate and mediate modes down to the very least spark of near-non-being, through all degrees of finiteness. Yet in each the primordial potency-in-act is expressed in appropriate form, and in the whole is undivided. In the phrase of Bruno, it is 'wholly in the whole, and wholly in every part of the whole'.[2]

It has often been claimed that a whole of parts must be divisible, and that if Nature is truly indivisible finite individuals can have no place in it. Spinoza must thus be either atheist or acosmist. This curious error arises from the interpretation of 'being' as 'thing' rather than as 'agent'. For the individuality of 'things' rests on exclusion, whereas that of 'agents' is enriched by mutuality, and in the end by it constituted. The manner of this constitution will become clear as we proceed.

Natura naturata, the actuality of Substantial potency-in-act is thus infinitely individuated, yet without division: it is an Individual of individuals to infinity. Here I must again enter a *caveat* against the common assumption that the finite modes of Substance are to be simply identified with the finite individuals of durational experience that come into being, endure, and pass away serially and contemporaneously 'from eternity to eternity'. For eternal *Natura naturata* can be no integration of such a stream of durational beings, nor these its differentiated parts. Thus, the problem that has gravelled so many of Spinoza's

[1] *Eth. I, xvi.*   [2] *De la causa, principio et uno, Dial. II.*

D

expositors and critics, as to how an eternal causality can, without self-limitation in the creator (which Spinoza denies, as entailing imperfection), give birth to durational effects, does not arise. The finite modes that are subordinate individuals in *Natura naturata* are themselves eternal as its constituents. Durational finite cona- tors are still far ahead in our exposition—though it must be allowed that Spinoza's own exposition in the *Ethics*, with its moralistic bias, does not sufficiently emphasize the essential gap. Here we are concerned with the eternal individuation of the mediate infinite and eternal mode of Substance, which must be conceived as an eternal macrocosm constituted hierarchically of microcosms to infinity, all of which are eternal as thus em- bedded.

Further, this individuation of the Individual is not *sub- division* or *section*, for thus *Natura naturata* would not be 'in- finite, unique, and indivisible' but indefinite, multiplex, and aggregate. Nor would its parts be actualizations of Substance, or analogues of Nature. Thus, our problem is set: the mediate infinite and eternal mode of Substance is the exhaustive actuality of the infinite, indeterminate, potency-in-act, fully determinate and individual; also it is constituted of infinite finite beings of all grades of perfection, each in its own measure actualizing the divine potency: under what *schema* is such a set of relations intelligible?

III. MACROCOSM AND MICROCOSMS

It must be admitted that Spinoza presents no formal unified account of the relations holding between *Natura naturata* and its finite 'parts'. Nor are suggestive terms such as 'macrocosm' and 'microcosm' much in evidence to yield a clue. Formal expression being lacking, his views must be sought out, and with a 'specu- lative eye'. Nor are the reasons for this *laches* far to seek: Spinoza is sometimes represented as among the purest of meta- physicians, for whom human values are only of secondary im- portance, but in fact his ethical interests are far too prominent to allow of such a characterization—though he is certainly a meta- physical moralist. Thus the *Ethics* contains much discussion of the nature, status, and moral relations of durational 'man', but all too little of 'man' as eternal *creatum*—and that little mainly, though far from exclusively to the perceptive reader, in the latter portion of *Part V* where, consequently, it has often seemed to the impercipient to be a superimposed and largely alien mystical efflorescence. But indeed, the nature of 'man' as perfect finite *creatum* (i.e. 'as referred to God') lies, as we shall see, at the very root of Spinoza's ethical doctrine, and he would have done better to have given distinct consideration to 'man's' eternal nature, not as a mere 'eternal part'[1] of the mind, but as its essential nature, and formally related the eternal natures of finite modes in general to the 'infinite, unique, and indivisible' nature of the divine actuality, passing thence to its variant immanence in the privative nature of durational beings. Even his moral doctrine might thus have been more acceptable to plain men.

But though we may regret Spinoza's 'moralism', we are not left wholly without guidance in our search for his metaphysical *schemata*. With the moralism there is very naturally coupled a one-sided emphasis on the human mind (and Spinoza expressly excludes from the *Ethics* the discussion of physical nature as such —beyond what is advanced in the physical *Lemmata* of *Part II*, and which concerns the nature and degrees of physical individuality, rather than the mode of integration of those degrees). It is therefore to the mental nature of 'man' (and his physical nature only as it is epistemologically involved in this), and its relation to 'God or Nature', that we have to look for the most promising clues. The human mind, he affirms, is the idea of the human body 'and nothing else';[2] yet also it can have adequate knowledge of the eternal and infinite essence of God;[3] and these propositions plainly imply that the nature of God is involved in human nature, and can be sought from it by some valid metaphysical procedure. 'God or Nature' is immanent in human nature.

But further, though the human mind is the idea of the human body, yet it can only know its nature, and even that it exists, in so far as it is 'affected' by other bodies;[4] and the natures and existence of those other bodies are known by the mind only in so far as they 'affect' its body.[5] From these propositions it follows that man's idea of the world of bodies is the idea of the 'affections' of his own body by all those other bodies; so that man's knowledge of nature depends on the capacity of his body to be

[1] *Eth. V, xxxix.*   [2] *Eth. II, xiii.*   [3] *Eth. II, xlvii.*
[4] *Eth. II, xix.* For *'affectio'* see above, p. 12.   [5] *Eth. II, xvi.*

'affected' by its complement in nature, and the resulting idea is inadequate in so far as it confuses the natures of the body and its bodily complement. Yet this confusion results only in so far as the body and its bodily complement are different in nature—not wholly different (for thus the body could not be 'affected' by its complement). In so far as they have 'common properties'[1] there can be no confusion; but in so far as their natures differ confusion is inevitable.[2] Thus the inadequacy of man's idea of nature is remediable, not by any process of analysing these confused 'affections' (for *ex hypothesi*, in separation neither body nor complement can be perceived by the mind), but only by the resolution of the differences in a full community of body and bodily complement in the '*facies totius universi*': 'he who possesses a body adapted to many things, possesses a mind the greater part of which is eternal.'[3]

It is thus full community of each finite being, up to the limits of its finiteness, with infinite *Natura naturata* that constitutes its eternal nature as *creatum*, and the eternal relation of the finite and the infinite is to be conceived, not as the resolution or absorption of the individual in a *totum* on the analogy of mere objective 'things' —man is no 'bubble of the foam' of Deity—but as congruent reciprocity on the analogy of co-operating agents. The finite *creatum* is an eternal agent or finite individualization of the eternal actuality of the divine agency—an active microcosm of the infinite active macrocosm, which is the hierarchical integration[4] of infinite such microcosmic agents, each of which is framed on the analogy of the whole. Yet because the macrocosm is infinite, and the microcosm only finite, the latter can only be framed on the *analogy* of the former, and the microcosm is an actualization of divine potency, not in so far as this is infinite and indeterminate, but only in so far as it is also actualized and self-determined in another finite agent—which also has reference to a third, and so to infinity.[5]

Let this brief sketch suffice to indicate the relations of finite and infinite active being as conceived by Spinoza. It remains to generalize it and set it forth in what seems the simplest and most telling way, viz. by means of a symbolic exposition. As this device is to be used merely as a clarification of relations already

---

[1] *Eth. II, xxxviii; xxxix.*   [2] See below, pp. 74–5.   [3] *Eth. V, xxxix.*
[4] See *Eth. II, Lem. vii, Sch.*   [5] Cf. *Eth. II, ix.*

conceived, and not as involving inference, even those who are not accustomed to place much confidence in symbolic procedures as means of attaining truth may find some advantage from its laconicism. Its simplicity, again, should reconcile those who do not work with ease in such a medium.

Let N stand for *Natura naturata* in its infinite integrity. Here we may ignore the distinctions of the Attributes as affecting the modes since individuation proceeds *pari passu* under all of them.

N is the infinite Individual composed of infinite finite individuals of every grade of perfection, so interwoven as to exclude all division from the whole. Let . . . , M_{n-2}, M_{n-1}, M_n, M_{n+1}, M_{n+2}, . . . stand for these finite individuals.

Consider the nature of any one of these finite individuals: it is not a 'part' of N in the sense of a 'sector'—for so, either it would be no 'individual', or N would be a mere aggregate. It is a finite expression of N, reproducing its infinite nature in some finite degree. Thus it is composed of 'parts' corresponding with the 'parts' of N. Let $M_n m_{n+1}$ stand for that 'part' of M_n that corresponds with M_{n-1}, etc., etc.

Then we have:

$$N = \int_0^\infty \begin{cases} \infty \\ \\ M_{n-2} = \int_0^\infty \ldots, M_{n-2}m_{n-2}, M_{n-2}m_{n-1}, M_{n-2}m_n, M_{n-2}m_{n+1}, \cdots \\ \\ M_{n-1} = \int_0^\infty \ldots, M_{n-1}m_{n-2}, M_{n-1}m_{n-1}, M_{n-1}m_n, M_{n-1}m_{n+1}, \cdots \\ \\ M_n = \int_0^\infty \ldots, M_n m_{n-2}, M_n m_{n-1}, M_n m_n, M_n m_{n+1}, M_n m_{n+2}, \cdots \\ \\ M_{n+1} = \int_0^\infty \ldots, M_{n+1}m_{n-2}, M_{n+1}m_{n-1}, M_{n+1}m_n, M_{n+1}m_{n+1}, \cdots \\ \\ M_{n+2} = \int_0^\infty \ldots, M_{n+2}m_{n-2}, M_{n+2}m_{n-1}, M_{n+2}m_n, M_{n+2}m_{n+1}, \cdots \\ \\ \infty \end{cases}$$

Consider next the relation between the 'part' of M_n that corresponds with M_{n-1} (viz. $M_n m_{n-1}$), and the 'part' of M_{n-1} that corresponds with M_n (viz. $M_{n-1} m_n$). Though these are evidently distinct (being 'parts' of individual agents of different grades of perfection) they are, within their diverse scopes, in active agreement; for as 'parts' of M_n and M_{n-1} analogous with M_{n-1} and M_n respectively, they share a common nature or 'property'. They are differentiated actualizations of an identical potency-in-act—and thus constitute nodes in the community of *Natura*. This may be symbolically illustrated if we abstract M_n (say) and its relatives in other 'parts' of N in our general picture, so as to indicate how it subsists by active community with its complement in *Natura naturata*. Thus:

$$
\begin{aligned}
&M_{n-2}\!\!\rightarrow \cdots\cdots\cdots, M_{n-2}m_n, \cdots\cdots\cdots\cdots\\
&M_{n-1}\!\!\rightarrow \cdots\cdots\cdots\nearrow, M_{n-1}m_n, \cdots\cdots\cdots\cdots\\
&M_n\!\!\rightarrow \cdots\ M_n m_{n+2}\!\!\leftarrow, M_n m_n\!\!\leftarrow\!\!\nearrow, M_n m_n, \ M_n m_{n+1}, M_n m_{n+2}, \cdots\cdots\\
&M_{n+1}\!\!\rightarrow \cdots\cdots\cdots, \ M_{n+1}m_n, \cdots\cdots\\
&M_{n+2}\!\!\rightarrow \cdots\cdots\cdots, M_{n+2}m_n, \cdots\cdots\cdots\cdots
\end{aligned}
$$

Each 'part', therefore, of N is the actuality of a grade of divine potency-in-act, so that it stands in community with all other 'parts' similarly defined. By this community alone, *as an agent and no mere 'thing'*, it maintains, and not loses by mergence, its individual being.[1] And the 'texture' of *Natura naturata* may thus be symbolized as an infinite 'web' or 'lattice' of which the infinite finite agents are the 'nodes' operating so as to form the indivisible integrity of the 'whole'. Thus, let m_{n-2}^{n-1} stand for the community or coaptitude of M_{n-1} and M_{n-2}, then we have:

---

[1] It has often been urged against Spinoza that the integrity of eternal *Natura* leaves no room for finite individuality, all finite modes being merged, without distinction, in the infinite whole. This is the inevitable result of the common failure to take due account of his explicit *activism*. Coapt *agents*, in proportion to their coaptitude, *maintain* their individuality, which is *constituted* by their community. *Natura* is not a 'thing', and its 'parts' are not *sectors* of a thing, but *microcosms* which, as finite expressions of the macrocosm, live by community with their congruent complement in the. macrocosm. Thus, their integrity enhances, not destroys, their individuality.

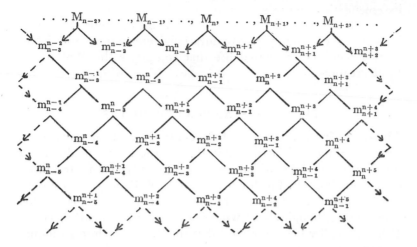

We have thus in *Natura* infinite hierarchical individuation of the perfect Individual—a macrocosm of microcosms to infinity. With Spinoza I have called the microcosms 'parts' of *Natura naturata* (as indeed, they are), yet each is nothing save as embedded in the whole which is undivided. When, therefore, we call the 'parts' finite (and I speak of the *eternal* 'parts') this does not deny to them all tincture of infinity. For each in perfect community with its congruent complement[1] in *Natura naturata*, in its degree expresses the infinite substantial potency-in-act; it is the actuality, not of God in so far as he is infinite, but in so far as he is considered as being 'affected' by its complement.[2]

Such, then, is the constitution of *Natura naturata* as it eternally actualizes the primordial potency-in-act, *Natura naturans*: 'infinite, unique, and indivisible', yet exhaustively differentiated in hierarchical order 'from highest to lowest'. It is this that forms the subject-matter of *Part I* of the *Ethics*, and the early propositions of *Part II*. It is to this also that Spinoza returns in the later propositions of *Part V*. Any failure to note that in these portions of his exposition Spinoza is dealing with eternal individuals in their constitutive community as they issue from the eternal potency or Substance, can produce nothing but confusion and futile misinterpretation. *Part II* is mainly concerned with the sources and status of the human mind as durational, *Part V* with

[1] See below, p. 48, note *.   [2] *Eth. II, ix.*

its emendation towards eternity, and *Parts III* and *IV* with its privative and impotent nature as unemended. Thus, he begins with eternal creation, passes to durational 'emanation', and thence to that recovery of eternal life that completes the 'dialectic of finite creation'.

IV. MODES AND ATTRIBUTES

There remains the problem of the contraction in the finite mode from the infinity of Attributes in the macrocosm to the duality of the Attributes under which 'man', e.g., our typical finite individual, finds himself. For 'man' is a mode of Thought and Extension exclusively.[1] This is a topic upon which Spinoza has far too little to say, though about which he is most pregnantly laconic. It has generally been assumed that the duality of human nature as animated body or embodied mind was for Spinoza a mere empirical *datum*, the infinity of the Attributes of Substance being the result of purely speculative 'principle-riding'. It is true, of course, that man's knowledge of his own nature as psychophysical is empirical, and not deduced from the nature of Substance, but his limitation to two Attributes, of which he is a duality in unity, is no mere *datum* but issues from the very nature and status of the Attributes which, as we have seen, are relative to 'intellect'. In Substance the Attributes are identical; in the perspective of intellect they are absolutely diverse, and each must be conceived through itself[2] as constituting the perceived essence of Substance. This being so, it follows that the modes of Substance which, for intellect, are discernible as determinations of diverse Attributes, are, as flowing from their substantial source, not separated under these Attributes but united; so that, e.g., man as mind and man as body are one man, not two living in miraculous harmony. If, now, it is thought that each mode of Substance should by intellect be discernible as a determination of all the infinite Attributes of Substance, and that therefore man cannot be limited to two Attributes, the error arises from failure to take due account of the nature and status of the Attributes. We are fortunate in having Spinoza's own answer to this problem (raised by his very acute correspondent von Tschirnhaus):[3] how

[1] *Eth. II, xiii, et Cor. et Sch.* On the nature of this limitation see below, p. 42, note 1.   [2] *Eth. I, x.*   [3] *Ep. lxv.*

does it come about that though each mode is expressed in infinite Attributes, the mode that is the human being knows only two of these—Thought as expressed in his mind, and Extension as expressed in his body. Spinoza's reply is brief and pointed: 'Although each thing is expressed in infinite ways in the infinite intellect of God, yet the infinite ideas by which it is expressed cannot constitute one and the same mind of a singular thing, but an infinity of minds: seeing that each of these infinite ideas *has no connexion with the others.*'[1]

Thus, (1) because the Attributes are wholly diverse in the perspective of intellect (a mode of one of them), one and the same mind must be united with *not more than one* other expression—since the remaining expressions cannot be intellectually incorporated; and (2) because the Attributes are relative to intellect there can be no mind that is *not* united with some other expression—for the mind knows itself only in the act of knowing something other than itself. For mind is not a 'thing' to which knowledge is superadded, but a *knowing agent*, and it must first be engaged in knowing something if it is to exist or be actual, and hence knowable. Nay, when the mind knows itself as knowing the body, it knows itself, not as a separate being, but as united with the body; and the union of mind and body is, from the standpoint of mind, *epistemic*. And this is the modal expression of the identity of the Attributes in Substance, and their relativity to intellect.[2]

It has often been claimed that in the system of Spinoza the Attribute of Thought is given a place pre-eminent among the infinite Attributes, in that it corresponds with *all* of them, and not, like the others, with *each* other. This is an objection that is hardly to be met by what has already been said about the union of minds with modes of other Attributes. Yet this pre-eminence of the Attribute of Thought is not to be wondered at in view of the relativity of the Attributes to intellect (which is a mode of Thought), and for philosophy (a human *intellectual* discipline) it is but an expression of the distinction of truth and reality. Here there is no idealistic evading of the paradox that though knowledge is *of* the real, the real transcends knowledge. But this intellectual pre-eminence of Thought affords no ground for an assertion of its *real* pre-eminence. In Substance the Attributes

---

[1] *Ep. lxvi* (my italics).   [2] But see below, p. 42, note 1.

are indiscerptible, and the distinction of union with *all* and with *each* other disappears. It is thus that the divine 'intellect', the actuality of substantial Thought (which is not other than substantial Extension, substantial X, etc.) 'resembles ours in nothing but in name. There could be no further likeness than that between the Dog in the heavens and the barking animal. . . . If intellect pertains to the divine nature it cannot, like our intellect, follow, nor be simultaneous with, the things that are its objects . . . but, on the contrary, the truth and real essence of things is what it is because as such it exists by way of knowledge in God's intellect.'[1]

---

[1] *Eth. I, xvii, Sch.* The scope of this book precludes a fuller discussion of the difficulties inherent in Spinoza's doctrine of the infinite Attributes of Substance, and of the restriction of human nature to two only of them, for in view of his laconic treatment of them any such discussion must place a greater reliance on rational speculation than is desirable in such an introduction. Nevertheless, for the sake of the more advanced, or more apt, reader, I will add the following remarks by way of clue.

The Attributes are distinct for intellect, but not in Substance itself, i.e. they form no infinite collection, but are discernible without falsification through the nature of modal intellect. Thus, on the one hand, to each true mode of Thought there is united a mode of Substance involving *every* Attribute, and on the other hand, since the Attributes, with their modes, are wholly distinct, and cannot be united to form a single systematic whole, to each true mode of Thought a mode of *one* Attribute only can be united. Addicts of 'the Yea and Nay of Elea' are apt to take this as constituting an irreconcilable contradiction. But this is to overlook the substantial, non-collective, unity of the Attributes, and, in particular, to misrepresent the manner in which such a unity must receive modal expression. The human intellect, e.g. is united with 'the body and nothing else', i.e. with a mode of Extension alone, and this is the manner in which the indeterminate unity of Substance is modally expressed in human nature. This modal union of Thought and Extension is thus in its way an expression of *all* the infinite Attributes, though a *positive* determination of two only. For determination is negation, the Attributes forming no *collection*, but the nature of each must be conceived, not as contrary to all others, but as their *inversion*; its determination *is* their negation. A rough analogy may be helpful to some readers (but must be used with great discretion): when white light falls on a thing that we perceive as red, the thing absorbs all the constituents of the white light except the red, which it reflects. The thing, therefore, is characterised, *in one way or another*, by all the constituents—its redness being a determination of whiteness involving, and made possible by, the absorption of the other constituents. In so far as white light is not a mere collection of coloured constituents, each colour may be regarded as the inverse of the remainder or complement. The analogy, of course, halts, but we may say that each Attribute of Substance is intellectually discernible from all others because its determinate nature is the inverse of the remainder. Now Thought is, for intellect, *other than* Extension, but it is not its *inverse*, for their union has a determinate character which is the inverse of a remainder. Thus a being uniting a mode of Thought with a mode of some Attribute other than Extension, could not be called a 'man', though it might express the same substantial potency under variant inversion, and therefore determination. For the primordial indeterminate substantial potency must be actualized, not merely in every possible way and finite degree, but in every possible concrete form or inversion. The question *why* man is limited to two Attributes only cannot, therefore, arise. For it is such a limited being that we call 'man,' and the limitation is intrinsic, not extrinsic. Determination not merely *implies* or *involves* negation, it *is* negation.

CHAPTER IV

DURATIONAL BEINGS

So far we have been concerned exclusively with eternal creation, and with finite individuals only as eternal microcosms in constitutive community 'from the highest to the lowest grade of perfection' in the 'infinite, unique, and indivisible' integrity of the eternal macrocosm, *Natura naturata*. Each finite agent in community with its complement is a finite expression of the infinite potency-in-act, *Natura naturans*, which is exhaustively actualized in the macrocosm. But the beings which come first in the order of human discovery are not eternal, perfect in their degree, indivisible, and necessary, but durational, privative, more or less isolated, and contingent. It is necessary, therefore, to give some account of the nature, etiology, and status of such beings, of the sempiternal 'common order of nature', and of their relations with eternal creation, finite and infinite.

I. FINITE MODES AS ETERNAL AND AS DURATIONAL

It must be admitted that this is a subject which is left by Spinoza himself in unusual obscurity—at least from the point of view of the modern mind, obstinately adhering to the principles of a truncated empiricistic positivism. The exposition of his doctrine has hitherto usually been taken alternatively as uncritically realistic or empirically sceptical, i.e. he has been thought either to offer no account at all of the relations of eternity and duration, or to have regarded durational finite beings as illusory; and this latter has been the view most commonly favoured. But indeed, it seems to me that both interpretations are incredible, and that the candid student should prefer to presume that the modern mind has lost the clue to this part of Spinoza's thought, so that an effort must be made to piece together his scattered assertions bearing reference to the subject, with their implications, so as to reconstruct his theory in the probable climate of his epoch and personal predilection. Doubtless, the effort must be 'speculative', but it need

not be fancifully speculative in the bad and unphilosophical sense
of that much-abused term. To avoid this speculative effort is not
only to minimize Spinoza's philosophical stature (which is perhaps a small matter), but to be involved in difficulties in the explanation of some of his most penetrating assertions, and to
suppose a double-mindedness, if not duplicity, in a thinker whose
most notable characteristic is singleness of mind in the pursuit of
truth. That he entertained no views on this absolutely crucial
subject, or that he did not recognize its incidence, might be conclusions forced upon us by failure in our effort—they cannot precede it; and that he held that the durational world is pure illusion
is contradicted by many overt statements, and by the whole tenor
of his ethical doctrine. Nor do I think that, once we have suc-
ceeded in placing ourselves at the viewpoint of Spinoza, his beliefs
are as occult, suppositious, or scattered in expression, as they may
prima facie seem to be without that advantage.

First, it must be noted that though there is a gulf fixed between
eternal and durational beings, the former being changeless, fully
communicant, and integral, while the latter are transient, separated, and at issue one with another, yet this is no impassable gulf,
since durational beings are not merely transient, but more or less
permanent (though coming into being and passing away), not
merely separated, but transeuntly related, not merely at issue one
with another, but more or less co-operative (born from the inter-
actions of others, preserved by the relative congeniality of their
environment, developing by their aptness for the utilization of
the powers of a world that is other than they). They are not mere
'clouds' of temporal 'events' but hold a middle position in the
scale of being. Thus it becomes possible to conceive them as eternal
beings 'under a cloud', degraded, weakened, and alienated. We
should have, then, to ask: What is the source of this degradation,
debility, and disharmony? Equally we should have to ask: What is
the source of their partial integrity, effort, and co-operation, in
virtue of which they endure? The answer to the first question in
terms of a relation with eternal being, will provide an answer to the
second: for if we can say what is the source of the division, debility,
and mutual alienation of durational beings, we shall be able to set
its limits, and to regard their partial integrity, effort, and co-operation as a remainder concomitant with the partiality of the descent
from eternal community towards temporal pulverulence.

Much of the misunderstanding and confusion that has infected expositions of Spinoza's thought on this subject may, perhaps, be attributed to that thought itself: we may here be dealing with a growing point that never reached full and explicit development. Thus in the *Cogitata Metaphysica*, though he defines 'creation' as 'an operation in which no cause is present but the efficient cause', and a 'created being' as 'one which presupposes for its existence nothing but God',[1] he nevertheless denies that any created being can be eternal: 'eternity can be attributed to God alone; not to any created being: not, I say, though its duration be without limit in both directions'.[2] The *Cogitata Metaphysica* is an early work, and furthermore is connected with Spinoza's exposition of the philosophy of Descartes; thus the doctrine may not be attributable to Spinoza—though if it is not, some hint of this would surely break through, or be noted with the other *caveats* in Dr. Meyer's *Preface*. If in creation no cause is operant but God, and God is eternal, it would seem to follow that created beings, too, must be eternal, and that enduring beings are not, as such, 'created'. It is noteworthy that in the *Ethics* very little use is made of the terms 'creation' and 'created being', and this seems likely to be connected with the recognition that durational beings, as such, are not unqualified derivatives of eternal potency-in-act. Yet the term 'creation' was too firmly established in common and theological thought as a relation of God and enduring beings to be freely used without great danger. The mere avoidance of a word, however, was more likely to conceal than to elucidate the issue; and what is lacking—and so easily and briefly might have been supplied—is a distinct, *ad hoc*, *Scholium* laying bare the implications of the doctrine of 'imagination' and its 'emendation', and unmistakably clarifying the relations of eternal agency and durational *conatus*.

II. THE DESCENT FROM ETERNITY

In so far as durational beings are centres of *effort* their authenticity[3] cannot be subject to doubt; for to be in any degree or manner active is in that degree or manner to be real.

---

[1] *Cog. Met.*, II, x.   [2] *Op. cit.*, II, i.

[3] I say 'authenticity' to avoid neologism: in truth, finite agents, eternal and durational, are 'synentic'—existing by relation, constitutive or auxiliary, with others.

1. *From Eternal Action to Durational Endeavour*

Consider, now, the eternal microcosm, reproducing in its finite scope the eternal macrocosm of which it is also a microcosmic 'part', acting in community with all others (i.e. its complement) up to the limits of its nature. In reproducing under limitations proper to its finite status the individuality of the macrocosm, it attains a relative individuality or selfhood as a distinct agent in the indivisible macrocosm. In virtue of this selfhood it is a 'frame of reference' in relation to which all other microcosms stand ordered and estimated. In this 'projection' of its complement in Nature upon its 'axes', this finite self-reference, that complement is partly obscured and distorted, so that the eternal community of *Natura naturata* is disorganized, and the self-referent microcosm discovers itself as at issue with a partially alien world. For it sets itself up as an extrinsic spectator of Nature, ignoring its implication in Nature as a created being, i.e. 'as referred to God'. Nor is this an illusion, or simple error, for the finite being is indeed a 'self', and its self-referent perspective of Nature a genuine 'projection', though eccentric, of its eternal complement. It and its world suffer privation only—not negation; and the privation is congruent with its degree of finiteness.

Popular thought has been wont to conceive creation as having taken place either in time, or at a supposed beginning of time, and to have been an action performed once for all, the created world continuing to exist through time under that original impulse. Descartes understood that such continuance in existence would require the creative action to be continually repeated, so that creation is to that extent posterior to time. Spinoza's position avoids the obvious difficulties inherent in all these views: for him creation is infinite and eternal action, and created beings are actualizations of divine potency, some infinite, and others finite in every possible grade of perfection. Critics have asked: how can finite durational beings be actualizations of potency infinite and eternal?—a question which receives only partial answer in terms of the conception of hierarchical individuation elaborated in the last chapter, which offers an explanation of the finite nature, but not of the durational nature, of the individual constituents of the world.

Spinoza's position is not to be gathered from the *Metaphysical*

Reflections appended to his early *Geometrical Version of Descartes's Principles of Philosophy* (which are confessedly largely Cartesian in form) for there eternity is said to belong to God alone, and not to created beings.[1] His developed doctrine, on the contrary, conceives created beings, whether finite or infinite, to be eternal, and durational beings fragmentary and confused privations of such eternal beings as 'projected' on the 'reference system' of the finite individual. Time, therefore, must neither be conceived as subsequent to creation nor as the scene of its continual operation, but the duration of a finite being in the sempiternity of the infinite world as a generalized privative exposition of its eternity.[2]

The eternal existence of the microcosm in the community of *Natura naturata*, and its durational life in a partially hostile world, must not, therefore, be taken as two lives, but the latter as an imperfect self-referent exposition of the former. In so far as the finite individual insists upon his selfhood, abstracting from his partiality, he refers his co-derivative complement in the macrocosm, not to their common cause, but to his own nature conceived, not as involved in Nature, but as a mere spectator. And thus he is self-involved in *metaphysical relativity*, and his eternity is debilitated to duration.[3]

---

[1] *Cog. Met. II, i.*

[2] Creation as it relates to the macrocosm is direct actualization of infinite potency; but as it relates to the microcosm, which though individual, is but a 'part' of the macrocosm, it is 'dialectical' in nature: integral selfhood and partiality being antithetical 'moments' in the finite creative synthesis. Under more or less exclusive self-reference, therefore, their synthesis is more or less adequate; and this variation in adequacy of synthesis of wholeness and partiality involves the privation of eternity as duration.

[3] Nor is it his *existence* only that is debilitated; for the very *essence* of being is obscured, and *agents* assume the mask of objective '*things*': that which by self-reference is occulted posits itself inversely as objective imaginational *datum*, i.e. as intellectual *ablatum*. Thus, by this 'projection' of its congruent complement in *Natura naturata** upon its own eccentric 'axes', that complement, which in the order of creation is in eternal community with the finite self, takes the form of a partially hostile other, and the finite self itself that of a struggling continuant

* By the 'congruent complement' of the finite self is meant the totality of the elements of all other finite beings in *Natura naturata* with which the elements of the finite self are in community. E.g., using the symbolism of pp. 37–40 above, the congruent complement of M_n is the totality of the 'parts': ..., $M_{n-2}m_n$ of M_{n-2}, $M_{n-1}m_n$ of M_{n-1}, $M_{n+1}m_n$ of M_{n+1}, $M_{n+2}m_n$ of M_{n+2}, ..., with which the 'parts' of M_n, ..., $M_n m_{n-2}$, $M_n m_{n-1}$, $M_n m_{n+1}$, $M_n m_{n+2}$, ..., are in community.

Durational being must thus be conceived as rooted in eternity, and issuing therefrom as a *nimbus* of partial impotency and inadequate actuality. Its duration as it thus issues, however, is not continuance in a pre-existing time, but itself determines its 'present' of potency-in-act, its 'past' of actuality, and a posited 'future' of promise. But this temporalization of naïve duration can be fully expounded only as we consider, not the isolated microcosm (for it lives by commerce with its other—as in eternity it exists in constitutive community with its complement), but this in relation with its partially dissonant field; and this qualification of our abstract account is worth separate consideration.

2. *Duration and Time*

Duration, says Spinoza, is 'the indefinite continuation of existing',[1] and he adds: 'I call it indefinite because it can in no wise be bounded by the nature of the existing thing itself, nor by its efficient cause which necessarily posits the existence of the thing, not annuls it.'[2] Yet though duration, as the efflux of the eternal existence of the finite microcosm as it refers its complement to its

operating in the 'field' of that other towards a satisfaction that its self-reference has disappointed. The essences of self and complement are partially occulted and confused through the screen or riddle of the self's finitude, and their existences 'telescoped-out' to the form of unsatisfied continuance or duration. Eternal community of agency is thus 'projected' as durational *conatus* in a conative 'field' which is only partially and variously co-operant. According to the grade of finiteness of the microcosmic self in *Natura naturata* its self-reference fragmentates and occults both itself and its congruent complement; and according to the degree of its emendation from self-reference to reference to God as *fons et origo*, eternal fruition is available to it even while it endures—no longer postponed as a durational 'end', but present in the act.

These remarks are addressed to the more mature student; and I will add that the 'dialectical' nature of finite creation must not be conceived as if its 'moments' were successive in time, for this would be mythology (which has its uses)† and not metaphysics. The antithetical 'moments' of eternal finite creation are, as it were, 'stresses' in a single action, and durational existence is this 'dialectic' of finite creation diffusively expounded, so that throughout duration both 'moments' are operative, though inadequately in this or that degree, and their synthesis is more or less eternal and durational. The eternal and the durational *parts* of the mind are not its *sectors*.

† Spinoza's own reference to eternal life as 'belonging to the duration of the mind without relation to the body' (*Eth. V, xx, Sch.*) and of the 'eternal part' of the mind as 'remaining' after the destruction of the body (*Eth. V, xxxiii*) are imaginational expressions of intellectual truths, and thus mythological.

[1] *Eth. II, Def. v.*   [2] *Eth. II, Def. v, Explic.*

E

own eccentric frame of reference, is not self-bounded, and may be conceived as indefinitely continuant under the patience of that external world of nature, or as bounded extrinsically, it is nevertheless implicitly temporal, issuing from a 'present' of conative potency-in-act, and by reason of the privative nature of its *conatus*, generating a receding 'past' of congruent actuality, and positing a vacuous 'future' of increasing fulfilment. The naïvest duration has a 'sense' which is implicitly temporal, and this remains tacit in Spinoza's term 'continuation'. When, now, we turn from the abstract consideration of the predicament of '*the* finite agent' to the more concrete consideration of that of '*this or that* finite agent' as he stands related to his complement in Nature, this implicit temporality of his duration is made explicit; for the durations of the things alienated by *his* self-reference (even in his perspective) are not bounded by his conative potency-in-act exclusively, but by *their* relative powers and degree of alienation. And this alienation may be either unilateral or mutual in various degrees (according as the self-reference involved is unilateral, mutual, or variously emended towards reference to God as *fons et origo* of all being). It is thus that the temporality of duration becomes explicit as the unilaterally or mutually bounded durations of things are compared as epochs of an indefinitely continuant duration in which all in their degrees and orders participate.[1] Duration is thus explicitly temporalized by this comparison of individual durations, and with precision by comparison 'with the duration of other things that have a fixed and determinate motion'.[2] Nevertheless, duration cannot be adequately conceived as *composed* of moments of time: 'If anyone conceived duration abstractedly, and, confusing it with time, began to divide it into parts, he would never be able to understand how, for example, an hour could pass.'[3] Duration is imaginational existence as indefinitely continuous, and time is its comparative measure as an 'aid to its imagination', not to its understanding. When, therefore, we speak of duration as 'explicitly temporal', it is its *actual* patience for subdivision and measurement, and not its conative *potency* as an indefinite efflux

---

[1] For the effluent durations of the multiplicity of finite agents stem privatively from sources which, as eternal, belong to the 'infinite, unique, and indivisible' eternity of *Natura naturata*, so that they emerge as epochs of a common duration subject to temporal measurement.

[2] *Cog. Met.*, I, iv.   [3] *Ep. xii.*

of eternity, that is asserted, And this actual patience stems from the 'implicit temporality' of its characteristic 'sense' or direction which is involved in its etiology.

III. ' REFERENCE TO GOD ' AND ' SELF- REFERENCE '

The key, then, to the explanation of the place of the finite durational being in *Natura naturata*, and its relation with its eternal finite reality as created therein, lies in the eccentricity and alienation entailed by the transference of the axes of reference from creative *Natura* itself, to the finite self of the created microcosm. As *creatum*, i.e. as issuing from the divine causality, and thus 'referred to God', the finite agent is at once individual and distinct yet integral to *Natura naturata*. In virtue of its distinct individuality it is a 'self' reproducing in its measure the selfhood of *Natura*, and can thus stand as a 'frame of reference' with respect to which its complement, as 'not-self', is referable. But in this projection, by reason of the self's finiteness and eccentricity (for the self is thus excluded from Nature as projected) both self and complement are pulverized and confused, and the eternal action in which they enjoy eternal community is debilitated to durational *conatus* more or less co-operative and obstructive. The integrity of *Natura naturata* is unequally divided, with the endeavouring self operating in a 'field' more or less hostile, and indefinitely surpassing the self in power. Eternal community is thus telescopically debilitated as a durational relation of self and not-self, partly co-operative (according to the place of the finite agent in the hierarchy of Nature) and partly hostile, so that final defeat is inevitable *sub specie durationis*. For 'there is no individual being in Nature which is not surpassed in potency and strength by some other being . . . by which it can be destroyed'.[1]

In the finite agent's self-referent perspective, therefore, transitory durational existence within the indefinitely continuant durational existence of nature comes to be imagined as its sole and inevitable destiny; and if man is disposed to fret at this fate it is because, by reason of his elevation in the hierarchy of Nature, his self-reference cannot wholly alienate him from his eternal reality. He 'feels and knows by experience that he is

---

[1] *Eth. IV, Ax.*

eternal'.[1] 'The cinders of his spirit glow in the ashes of his chance', because he cannot altogether ignore his nature as an expression of Nature—his durationality and *conatus* registering only the fragmentation and debilitation of the expression, not its total pulverization and negation. Indeed, that the life of the self-referent agent is durational at all is due to the partial co-operation of self and not-self, which abstractedly expresses, *sub specie durationis*, the eternal community of finite agent and complement in *Natura naturata*. And though its duration is limited in both directions by the 'impatience' of its alienated complement, yet its eccentricity cannot wholly alienate it from 'itself, and God, and things', though it can, and does, cast a cloud over them, which can be dispersed only by passage from self-reference to 'reference to God' by which the integrity of creation is achieved.

IV. THE ONTOLOGICAL STATUS OF DURATIONAL BEINGS

Yet this recession from the 'reference to God' proper to eternal creation, to self-reference and the emanation of durational existence, is not alien to the creative process as it concerns the finite agent who is, indeed, an individual with a proper selfhood finitely reproducing the Individual Self: it is a 'moment' in the dialectic of the creation of the finite, and thus nature as 'projected' on the finite 'frame of reference' is not mere illusion. Nor is the 'common order of nature' the product of error, save in so far as it is taken as incorrigible both in its durationality and in its *de facto* pulverulence. Thus also, though eternity as it flows from the essence of the eternal being is existence *par excellence*, duration is a genuine form of existence. Nay, even its implicit temporality as concretely effluent cannot detract from its genuineness, though in so far as it is sophistically reduced to time it must be destroyed. Theories which make of duration any kind of series of instantaneous moments do but 'take pains to rave with the imagination'.[2]

I have said that the durational conator and its world are not mere illusions or products of error. Imaginations 'are not opposed to truth, nor do they vanish with its presence'.[3] This

[1] *Eth. V, xxiii, Sch.*   [2] *Ep. xii.*   [3] *Eth. IV, i, Sch.*

accords even with common experience: though we know that the trees on the distant hill are green, they still look grey; and though we know that the sun is many millions of miles away, it still looks much nearer;[1] and the appearances can be explained in such a way as to maintain without paradox their genuineness (though relativity as appearances). Similarly, with eternal and durational existences: they are different 'perspectives' of identical agents. Not, however, that any simple 'one-to-one' relation can be asserted between common-sense things and eternal agents; for the former are imaginational, and their common-sense boundaries set as 'things' rather than as 'agents', so that durational agency is fragmented, dispersed, and confused. For not all, if any, discernible spatio-temporal things, for example, are isolable as durational agents, though durational agents may be apprehended as endeavouring organizations of spatio-temporal factors. Conative pseudo-individuality is the characteristic of genuine durational beings as self-referent perspectives of eternal finite agents; and such imaginational beings cannot be said to be false, fictitious, or chimerical—save in so far as they are taken to be real without qualification or metaphysical derivation. The doctrine of 'degrees of reality' must thus be understood as implying, not degrees of 'givenness', but degrees of centricity in projection, or of adequacy in the expression of creative action. Thus also, the finite *creatum* may be said to have both an eternal and a durational 'part', so long as these are not regarded as *co-ordinate sectors* symmetrically related. It exists eternally 'as referred to God', but as a finite self, by referring its complement to its own 'axes' it emanates a *nimbus* of durational existence under the 'patience' of its more or less alienated complement, and bounded by its 'impatience'. For birth, and vicissitude, and death are functions of *unsubordinated* self-reference.

---

[1] *Eth. II, xxxv, Sch.; IV, i, Sch.*

PART II

THE DOCTRINE OF KNOWLEDGE

CHAPTER V

IDEAS AND *IDEATA*

Spinoza's epistemological doctrine is expounded at some length in the *Tractatus de Intellectus Emendatione*, and more briefly in *Ethices II*, where it takes its place in the general view of man and the world and God there set forth—receiving in *Part V* its ultimate philosophical enucleation. In its broadest interpretation, epistemology is for Spinoza metaphysics conceived as concerned with the nature of mental being as the actuality of the Attribute of Thought, but as thus focused upon the modes of one Attribute (discernible only by modal intellect) the 'knowledge' with which it is concerned is primarily modal in form, i.e. knowledge as it pertains to the human mind, not divine or substantial knowledge which differs from it, in his well-known phrase, as the Dog-star from the barking animal. It is from human knowledge, therefore, that Spinozistic epistemology begins—indeed, in the *Tractatus* (as its title indicates) from empirical human percipience as it demands emendation for the elimination of error, dubiety, and mere fancy. In the *Ethics*, too, by reason of its ethical intention, human knowledge remains central—*Part II* passing, not to the nature of Thought and its modes in general, but to the nature of the mind, i.e. the human mind.[1] Yet Spinoza never conceived human knowledge, even as 'emended' so as to exclude all error, dubiety, and fancy, as anything more than a finite modal expression of the substantial identity of Thought and its coordinate Attributes. The duality of mind and its primary object belongs to the modal intellectual perspective, not to creative Substance. The naïve empirical notion, therefore, of knowledge as being a *relation*, whether of compresence of mind and object, or of representative idea and extrinsic thing represented, must be fundamentally misleading if taken as exemplary. Knowledge is by nature wholly mental, and the congruent compresence of

---

[1] It is the ethical intention of the work, too, that turns the attention of the philosopher in *Part II*, not to the nature and origin of the whole *finite individual*, but to the nature and origin of *the human mind*.

mind and object, and the presentation of thing by mind, alike
stem from the substantial identity of the Attributes. In knowledge the mind does not contemplate its relation with its object
from some neutral standpoint: it *is* the apprehension of its object.
The *action* of knowing[1] is its very essence, and knowledge is the
actuality of its essential potency.

Consider, then, the human mind: it is a knowing agent, i.e. it
is the apprehension of an object. This *object*, by the knowledge
of which it is individual, is identified by Spinoza with the human
body which, as the mind's object, is its extended *correlate*.[2] The
correlation of mind and body is, indeed, their *union*,[3] and a
modal expression of the substantial identity of Thought and
Extension—their distinction being a modal expression of the
intellectual distinction of these Attributes. Critics have been
quick to object that Spinoza's identification of the mind's *object*
with its *correlate* conflicts with common experience—the mind's
bodily correlate (viz. some part of the brain) and its object (which
is external, or at least peripheral) being always distinct. But this
objection is founded upon an uncritical acceptance of the adequacy of empirical percipience. The human body *as it is in act*,
i.e. as united with the human mind, is not as it is perceived *ab
extra*.[4] Such empirical perception is, for Spinoza, but a species of
confused pseudo-cognizance. Just as 'the sordid images that are
the mind'[5] are but a cloud upon its nature, so also the 'feather-
less biped' of common experience must not be taken as the body's
original. The truth of common experience must be *concluded*, *not
premised*, in an adequate epistemology; it is premised only as
problematic and thus corrigible.

I. IDEAS, THEIR TRUTH, AND THEIR ADEQUACY

An 'idea', it has been said, is a mode of think*ing*, or of mental
action, i.e. it is a potency-in-act. Locke's notion, therefore, of an
idea as 'the object of the understanding when a man thinks'[6] is

---

[1] It is often said today that knowing is not an 'action'. This opinion appears to
stem from misconception of the nature of 'action' as essentially durational.
Knowing is, of course, not a durational *process*, though learning may be.

[2] *Eth. II, xi; xiii.*   [3] *Eth. II, xiii, Sch.*

[4] See above, p. 6. On the supposed fallacy of Spinoza's identification of the
mind's object and correlate, see my article: 'On a Reputed Equivoque in the
Philosophy of Spinoza' (*Review of Metaphysics*, iii, pp. 189–212).

[5] T. S. Eliot.   [6] *Essay, I, i.*

remote indeed from the conception of Spinoza; and though
Spinoza does describe an idea as the 'objective essence' of the
thing ideated, this must not be interpreted as signifying that it is
an objective[1] mental entity congruent with, or representing, the
thing cognized. On the contrary, it signifies that the idea *presents*[2]
the thing as *ideatum* or object, and the '*formal* essence' of the idea,
what it is in itself, is this action of presenting.

When Spinoza describes an idea as the 'objective essence' of its
ideatum or object,[3] though to the unwary post-Lockeian this may
suggest that it is an objective mental thing reproducing in another medium the content of the *ideatum*, the suggestion is false
because it ignores the distinct ways in which the abstracted content is related to ideas and to *ideata*, viz. 'objectively' or ter-
minally to the former, and attributively to the latter. Instead of
saying, with Descartes, that the thing ideated is 'contained objectively'[4] in the idea of the thing, less ambiguously I shall say

---

[1] Although it is now generally understood, the reader must beware of the ambiguity that attaches to the term 'objective' by reason of its contrasted scholastic
and post-Kantian senses. Spinoza uses the term in its scholastic sense (which I
have generally indicated by quotes); but the later sense can hardly be avoided
in a modern exposition (especially as Spinoza himself uses 'object' and '*ideatum*'
interchangeably). The scholastic term 'objective' is contrasted with 'formal',
i.e. real (a use derived from Plato), and bears reference to ideas as distinct from
their objects or *ideata*; the post-Kantian term 'objective' is contrasted with 'sub-
jective', i.e. mental, and bears reference to *ideata* or objects as distinct from
ideas.

[2] Not '*represents*' or 'takes the place of'. It is too often assumed that the
Latin '*repraesentare*' is equivalent to '*ad vicem accedere*', whereas 'immediate
presentation' is its primary sense.

[3] Descartes distinguished the 'formal (or material) reality' of an idea from its
'objective reality' (*Meditationes, Praef.*), i.e. the action of cognizing from its
modality as being the cognizing *of this or that particular being*. Formally (or
materially) as mental action, all ideas are 'equal' (*Meditationes, III*), but objectively they are widely diverse. It is by the nature of the objects presented by
ideas that ideas are discernible. Yet it does not follow that distinct ideas are
objective presentations (as some Cartesians assumed, following some suggestions
of Descartes himself, speaking as a psychologist, and not as a philosopher—for
the contemporary confusion of philosophical and scientific inquiry is the source
of much Cartesian ambiguity). Descartes himself, *qua* philosopher, was quite
clear that an idea is an *operation* of the mind, and not an objective ideal content.
An idea is not a ghostly simulacrum, or representative, of its *ideatum*, but the
mental operation that *terminates* in it. (Cf. *Meditationes, Resp. ad Sec. Obj.,
Deff. i-iii.*)

[4] But note Descartes's own explanation of this otherwise ambiguous phrase
in *Resp. ad Sec. Obj., Def. ix.*: 'When we say that something is contained in the
nature or concept of anything, that is precisely the same as saying that it is true
of that thing, or can be affirmed of it.'

that as its epistemic *terminus* the *ideatum* modalizes the idea or mental action.

Such being the general nature of ideas: mental *actions*, not mental *things*, consider next Spinoza's account of the 'true idea' and the nature of its 'truth'. We have seen that an idea is not true by reason of its congruence with 'fact': blind guesses may agree with 'facts', but they are *lucky* rather than *true*. Furthermore, we have no means of comparing ideas with 'facts', for facts are only known by means of ideas. The certification of truth must lie within the nature of ideas, 'facts' being established by the truth of ideas, and not the truth of ideas by appeal to 'facts'.

The problem of truth thus concerns the manner in which the true idea is recognized and certified. This must be by reference, Spinoza says, not to the 'extrinsic' but to the 'intrinsic denominations' of the idea. The true idea is the idea that is intrinsically *adequate*, and by this it is certified as true. But the nature of this 'adequacy' needs careful attention. Joachim's account of it, e.g., largely misses the point by reason of alien presuppositions: 'What constitutes . . . the adequacy . . . of knowledge is its inner coherence—the clarity and distinctness of the elements of its content, and the logical necessity of their connexions.'[1] This well-known 'coherence-theory' of truth, however, is commonly conceived in terms of objective 'ideal content' and so misses what is central in Spinoza's theory, viz. the intrinsic *agency* of ideas. Thus 'adequacy' comes to be identified with inner coherence of 'ideal content'. for which agreement with 'fact', i.e. an 'external counterpart', is supererogatory, and epistemically a mere accident.[2] But for Spinoza, this agreement is no accident though it does not *constitute* truth; and although adequate ideas are certainly coherent, this coherence does not constitute their adequacy: fictions may be coherent.[3]

Wherein, then, lies the 'equality' in virtue of which an idea is said to be 'ad-equate'? It is not the equality of objective 'ideal content' and *ideatum*; nor that of a whole of 'ideal content' with

---

[1] *Commentary*, p. 92. It is true that Joachim stresses again and again that an idea is an '*act*' of mind, an affirmation, a judgement—but always as -ed without -ing, as referr*ed* 'ideal content'. But an -ed without an -ing is a chimera.

[2] *Op. cit.*, p. 94.

[3] So far as they go—hence the Bradleian resort to the idea of the coherent *whole*. But for Bradley this is not 'true', but identical with its supposed object.

its elements as coherently assembled. Indeed, abstracted from the action of the mind which it modalizes, or from the thing which it characterizes, the 'ideal content' is a mere abstraction and thus no *tertium quid* distinct both from the knowing mind and the known thing, realistically mediating the latter to the former, or idealistically usurping the place of the latter. It has being only as modalizing the mental action, or as characterizing the thing, i.e. as mental action *qua* idea *of that thing*, or that thing *qua ideatum*. The adequate idea *presents* the thing as *ideatum*, not *re*presents it as 'ideal objective content'. For mind is not a ghostly *thing* but a knowing *agent*, and in true knowledge it is the real that is known.

The adequacy of an idea lies, therefore, in its intrinsic nature as a distinctly directed mental action or potency-in-act; and the equality in virtue of which it is 'ad-equate' is that of its actuality as 'idea of X', with the potency posited as its source. It is thus that the idea of the *causa sui* is adequate and self-certifying *par excellence*. But the potencies that ideas of finite beings actualize, are only derivative, so that the equality then lies between the actuality of the 'idea of X', and the potency of its postulated 'proximate cause'. The simplest examples of this principle (apart from metaphysical ideas which, at this stage, may be disputed by the unconvinced) are to be found among the rational ideas of mathematics,[1] and Spinoza's own examples are geometrical. For instance, the idea of the sphere as actualized by the potency of the semicircle rotating about 'a centre'[2] (i.e. its diameter) is adequate, the potency inherent in, and supplied to, the semicircle to constitute the 'proximate cause' of the sphere, being equal to its actuality. This, he says, is the easiest way of forming the concept of the sphere,[3] which, in itself is but an *ens rationis*, and 'forms the essence of no individual thing',[4] yet

---

[1] Empirical examples are not merely hard to come by, but if found would be *nihil ad rem* by reason of the durational nature of empirical things, and the transeuncy of their proximate empirical causes. Again, the mathematical nature of Spinoza's examples does not invalidate them, for the objects of mathematics, though *entia rationis*, are not Humian 'relations of ideas', but 'common properties' of *entia realia*, having 'a will of their own' to which the mathematician is subject—not 'formally' but 'objectively' in the elaboration of true mathematical ideas. He who imagines that circles and triangles are 'mere ideas' has not begun to understand the nature of ideas.

[2] *Tract. de Intell. Emend.*, § 72.

[3] *Loc. cit.*

[4] *Eth. II, xxxvii.*

'exists in nature'[1] as a 'common property' of certain singulars otherwise differentiated. The rotational potency must be *supplied* to the semicircle, since it is not proper to it,[2] and the remainder of the potency actualized in the sphere is already actual as the semicircle. Thus, though the idea of the rotating semicircle is itself inadequate, since there is no power in the semicircle in virtue of which it rotates, the idea of the sphere in terms of the semicircle *made* to rotate, is adequate by reason of the equality of the actualized sphere with the potency inherent in, plus that supplied to, the rotating semicircle. In other words, the idea of the sphere is adequate because the concept is equal to what is affirmed. The adequate idea is the *self-active* idea, though its self-activity may not be primordial (as with the idea of the *causa sui*) but derivative from a partially actualized 'proximate cause' (as with the idea of the sphere).

In general, then, the adequate idea is one that affirms no more than can be actual by reason of the potency postulated[3]—that affirms no 'effect' for which 'causes' are not adduced, either as of intrinsic right (as with the idea of the *causa sui*) or through mediation (as with finite things).[4]

---

[1] *Eth. II, vii, Sch.*

[2] The only rotational potency that is inherent in the semicircle is that in one plane by a line fixed at one end.

[3] If I affirm that 'Peter exists' without adequate grounds, then even though Peter does exist, my idea is inadequate—it is false, 'or if it be preferred so to speak, it is not true' (see *Tract. de Intell. Emend.*, § 69). Certain knowledge of existence can be achieved only in so far as its potency is actualized in the self-certified existence of the knower himself—so far at least Spinoza is at one with Descartes. But the issues are confused in so far as it is Peter's *durational* existence, or presence, that is in question. For here it is 'fact' or 'evidence', rather that 'truth' (see below, pp. 83–5) that must be decided; and the idea of the durational existence, or presence, of Peter can at best be 'evident', not 'adequate' —the absence of such 'evidence' rendering the idea suppositious rather than 'factual'. The principles are broadly parallel, and connected, but not identical. I have *adequate* knowledge of the existence of Peter in so far only as the imaginational 'evidence' of his presence is emended to the form of co-dependence on a common cause or potency, so that Peter and I are in perfect community—and this is partly achieved in love, in sodality, and even in debate.

[4] But not by transeunt production (as with durational things), for here full adequacy, as distinct from 'evidence' or 'fact', would involve reference to an indefinite series and assemblage of transeunt causes; and thus, in principle, be unrealizable. The 'proximate causes' required for adequate ideas of finite beings are immanent, not transeunt.

II. *IDEATA* AS THINGS AND AS AGENTS

Though the truth of an idea is thus its intrinsic adequacy, this principle involves no denial of the congruence of idea and *ideatum* as characteristic of truth. The 'extrinsic denomination' of the true idea is not *denied* by Spinoza. Yet because an idea is not a mental 'thing', but a mental *action* discernible, but not constituted, by the nature of its *ideatum* or *terminus*, it follows that the congruence of idea and *ideatum* cannot be merely objective. Idea and *ideatum* are not two things having the same objective form in different materials. Their congruence thus requires that the *ideatum*, like the idea, is an *agent* and not a mere 'presentation'. *It is the agency of real beings that distinguishes them from mere presentations.* What distinguishes the *ideatum* from the idea is the nature of their agencies (e.g. as mental or physical), i.e. the natures of the potencies (or Attributes) of which they are actualizations (or modes). And that which modalizes the mental action as *that* idea, characterizes the physical being as *that ideatum*, but apart from the modalization and the characterization is but an *ens rationis*.

Thus, just as the idea of a physical being is mental action discernible as being the limited action of cognizing *that* being, so the *ideatum* of the idea, viz. the physical being, is physical action discernible as being *that* limited potency-in-act. The congruence of idea and *ideatum* is of their agencies limited equally but diversely according to the nature of the agency.

How, indeed, could a real being be distinguished from a presentation save by reason of its distinct agency? The very root of the Berkeleian idealism lies in the assumption that all agency is mental, and the Johnsonian refutation of it lies in the insistence on the reality of agency that is not mental but physical.[1] One of the oddest aberrations of historical 'empiricism' is its failure to take note of what lies at the heart of all 'experience', viz. enjoyment of agency, mental and physical—its 'radical objectivism'. 'Presentations' become 'bodies', and 'ideal contents' become 'minds' only as each is rightly associated with the agencies, physical or mental, by which they are 'realized'. Nor are these 'presentations' and 'ideal contents' positive augmentations of the

[1] See my article 'Dr. Johnson's Refutation of Bishop Berkeley' (*Mind*, N.S. lvi, pp. 132–47).

respective agencies which are the essences of body and of mind, but declensions registering by their passivity as such, the limitations suffered by mental and physical relative isolation.[1]

The correspondence of idea and *ideatum* when the idea is adequate stems therefore from the substantial identity of the Attributes of Thought and Extension as primordial potencies-in-act. It is a correspondence of two forms of agency discernible only in the perspective of modal intellect. The objectivity that limits the mental action, and that which limits the physical action, do not *correspond*, but are identical abstractions or *entia rationis*.[2] In the true idea, mind and its physical world are epistemically compresent directly, without *interpositum*. And this is as true of limited ideas of limited physical beings, in which the mental and physical agents are congruently determined in the manners suited to their agencies, as it is of perfect knowledge which suffers no such limitation, and which Spinoza calls 'intellectual love'. It is thus that the idea is the 'objective essence' of its *ideatum*.

III. INADEQUATE IDEAS, THEIR NATURE AND STATUS

But though in the strictest sense only ideas which are adequate and true constitute 'knowledge', Spinoza shows no disposition wholly to deny epistemicity to ideas that fall short of perfect adequacy. Just as for him knowledge that is partial is nevertheless genuine, so that truth is not confined to the idea of being, perfect, infinite, and eternal, so also ideas of things contingent and corruptible are not forms of mere nescience, pure and simple, but, rightly regarded, find their appropriate place in the scale of knowing. It is thus alone that defence is forthcoming for the 'analytical' method in metaphysics by procedure from 'evident' ideas of beings (thus 'factual' or 'authentic' in the popular sense)

---

[1] It is the agency, including that which suffers declension, and not the declension as such, that constitutes the reality of finite beings:

'All I could never be,
'All, men ignored in me,
'This, I was worth to God, whose wheel the pitcher shaped.'

[2] A truth crudely infecting the theory which falsely regards 'sense-*data*' as *parts* of the physical thing. Falsely, because neither, conceived as passive object, has real being. The *data* of sense and the 'objects' of sense are unreal abstractions from the epistemically compresent mental and physical agents, not separate entities.

by emendation to 'true' ideas of beings 'authentic' in the proper
or etymological sense of self-generating.

The elucidation of the nature and status of inadequate ideas is
founded on the metaphysical principles already outlined in Chapter IV,[1] where the relations of eternal and durational existence
were traced to the distinction between creational 'reference to
God' and the unilateral finite self-reference of the microcosmic
individual which, unemended, involves its nature in privation,
both physical and mental. A fuller account of the sources and
nature of the inadequacy of the ideas of common experience
must be postponed to a later chapter,[2] but here it may be said in
general that inadequate ideas are the expression of the mental
privation that results from the 'projection' of the finite individual's complement in Nature upon its eccentric 'axes', by which
that eternal complement is apprehended, not as it is in itself as a
divine *creatum*, but as it stands related to the finite being self-impoverished by relative self-isolation. In the eternal stream of
creation the finite individual has being in so far as it holds community with its complement in the infinite Individual; but that
being, as individual, provides its own 'frame of reference', and,
as finite, operates as a 'screen' in relation to which, not only is
the indivisible and eternal complement (as embedding the finite
individual) distorted as an 'other', divided and temporal, but also
impoverished under the category of 'thinghood', so that it is projected as more or less alien (according to the status of the self-referent finite individual), and the individual itself, which exists
only by relation with its complement, suffers a congruent degradation as thus relatively self-isolated. Its eternity and finite perfection in the integrity of *Natura naturata* are distorted and
clouded, and can only be restored and clarified by a transition
from unilateral self-reference to reference to God. Inadequate
ideas are thus the progeny of finite self-reference; and they are
epistemic as the ideas of the distorted and impoverished 'projections' of the eternal real—ideas which, though not truly
'authentic' or eternally self-acting, may nevertheless be durationally 'evident' or 'factual', not to be rejected as mere illusions or
modes of nescience. With such 'evident' ideas, illusion arises
only from failure to regard their relative status, or the nature and
degree of their metaphysical relativity.

[1] Especially Sections iii–iv.   [2] See below, Chapter VII.

F

But though such ideas *may* be 'evident', not all inadequate ideas enjoy this epistemic quasi-perfection: unilateral finite self-reference so distorts and impoverishes the mind that no wholly 'evident' or 'factual' substitute for eternal *Natura* can be forthcoming. The mind is distracted by error, doubt, and fancy so long as it remains unemended. Yet these too can be understood—or their unintelligibility made intelligible (as the inevitable hazards of finite being) by the light of sound reason. For no idea, however imperfect, is wholly nescient, though its epistemicity may be parasitical. But to these further topics we shall return in Chapter VII.

IV. 'IDEAS OF IDEAS'

Just as the human mind knows only the human body,[1] yet knows that body only as it is 'affected' by other bodies in nature,[2] and thus also has knowledge of those other bodies, though only through these '*affectiones*',[3] so also the mind can reflect only on itself, though other minds in nature, as 'affecting' it, are thus, through these '*affectiones*', involved in its reflection on itself. But the mind's knowledge of itself is of itself as knowing the body, so that each idea is a doubly epistemic action or endeavour, having both a primary and a reflexive object. The mind's knowledge which is primarily and directly knowledge of the body involves, by its very nature as 'knowledge', knowledge of itself which is secondary and reflexive. Its knowledge of itself, however, is of itself *in act*, i.e. *as knowing the body*, for without a direct and primary object, distinct from itself, there would be no actual mind, or knowing agent, to know.[4]

For one reason or another students of Spinoza have been apt to make hard going of his doctrine of reflexive knowledge or *idea ideae*. Joachim in particular not only assigned to it a unifying function that it cannot, and was never intended to, fulfil,[5] but also directed against it criticisms which have their source in misin-

---

[1] *Eth. II, xiii.*   [2] *Eth. II, xix.*   [3] *Eth. II, xvi, Cor. ii.* See above p. 35.
[4] Cf. *Eth. III, ii, Sch.*, where the notion of 'unconscious mind' is attributed to the operation of the body without the inclusion in the empirical mind of the concomitant mental awareness. For the epistemic correlation of mind and body is obfuscated under unilateral finite self-reference. Indeed, it is thus that the mind's empirical 'object' and 'correlate' are separated, while its real object *is* its correlate.
[5] *A Study of the Ethics of Spinoza*, pp. 140 *et seq.*

terpretation and alien presupposition.[1] Taken in isolation, if its punctuation is ignored, a certain ambiguity may be found in Spinoza's formal statement that '*idea ideae, nihil aliud est quam forma ideae, quatenus haec ut modus cogitandi, absque relatione ad objectum consideratur*',[2] since the phrase '*absque relatione ad objectum*' may be taken either as adjectival, qualifying '*modus cogitandi*', or as adverbial, qualifying '*consideratur*'. Joachim, supposing the former, objects that such reflexion so 'impoverishes' the idea as to deprive it of what is essential to it, viz. its 'reference to an object', so that there remains but a 'knowledge so indeterminate and general that by it nothing in particular is known'.[3] But such a reading is incredible in view of Spinoza's own statement in the very work with which Joachim was concerned, that ideas are the 'objective essences' of things, and again, that in order to know that I know anything, I must first know it,[4] so that the possibility of taking a mode of thinking 'without relation to its object' is plainly excluded. But we may nevertheless *consider* it as 'something intelligible *per se*',[5] distinct from its object, and having its own 'formal essence' as exclusively mental; and the phrase 'without relation to its object' must therefore be taken (and as the punctuation suggests) as adverbial, qualifying '*consideratur*'.

Spinoza's position is thus that the primary 'idea of X' is a mental mode distinct from 'X' (the physical mode of which it is the idea), and that as such it has exclusively mental being—not as 'some idea or other', but as the 'idea *of X*'—in which is involved, in the very act of *being* that idea, the *consciousness* of being it. From this consciousness is excluded, not the epistemic relation to 'X', but 'X' itself. To use the phraseology of *Ethices II, Def. iv et Explic.*, the *idea ideae* is knowledge of the epistemicity of the idea as an 'intrinsic' and not an 'extrinsic denomination'. And it is thus that the real concern of reflexive knowledge is not the *correspondence* of the idea with its physical object, nor its mere ideal *coherence*, but its *adequacy or inadequacy*: *it is an idea of self-appraisement*. Hence, Spinoza makes it the foundation of his

---

[1] See *A Study of the Ethics of Spinoza*, pp. 138–40. [2] *Eth. II, xxi, Sch.*
[3] *Spinoza's* Tractatus de Intellectus Emendatione, *A Commentary*, pp. 105–7. It is only fair to say that, following these criticisms, Joachim proceeds to an account of the corrections which he desiderates, and in so doing largely points to Spinoza's own doctrine (see *Commentary*, pp. 108–11).
[4] *Tract. de Intell. Emend.*, § 34. [5] *Op. cit.*, § 33.

doctrine of philosophical method: 'the method is nothing but reflexive knowledge or the idea of the idea; and because there is no idea of an idea unless first there is an idea, therefore unless first there is an idea there is no method'.[1]

The doctrine of *idea ideae* is thus both an expression of the *nature* of mind as essentially *self-conscious* consciousness of the body, and also of its proper *function* as the epistemic *appraisement* of its primary work. Nature and function are, of course, essentially connected: it is because, in knowing, the mind is no mere passive mirror or impressionable plate, but an agent conscious of its agency, that it is also by nature capable of improvement. And it is in this effort of self-emendation that the mind discovers its true nature.

It is in terms also of this double concern of the doctrine with both nature and function that the question of the identity or distinction of the '*idea*' and the '*idea ideae*' must be resolved. In the *Tractatus de Intellectus Emendatione* Spinoza emphasizes the distinction of the idea and its object: 'a true idea is something different from its object';[2] and the presumption is that the *idea ideae*, therefore, though also an 'idea', is distinct from the idea which is its object—a conception which suggests an indefinite series of reflexive ideas of ideas, ideas of ideas of ideas, etc., distinct in nature, rather than self-conscious identity: the 'idea of Peter' is one idea, and the 'idea of that idea of Peter' is another. In the *Ethics*, however, he states that the distinction of the 'true idea of X' from 'X' itself lies in their being modes of different Attributes, viz. of Thought and Extension; whence it follows that the 'true idea of the idea of X' is identical with the 'true idea of X', since 'both' are modes of the same Attribute, viz. of Thought; 'he who knows anything, *by that very fact* (*eo ipso*) knows that he knows it, and also (*simul*) knows that he knows that he knows, and so to infinity'.[3] These statements, however, it must be noticed, refer to the human mind and body as they 'exist in God' and 'follow from him',[4] i.e. as eternal *creata*, and though they are in a manner applicable to the mind and body as 'confused and mutilated' by self-reference in the 'common order of nature',[5] it can only be with qualification. For where the primary 'idea of X' is *inadequate*, the 'idea of the idea of X' is not necessarily

---

[1] *Tract. de Intell. Emend.*, § 38.   [2] *Loc. cit.*   [3] *Eth. II, xxi, Sch.*
[4] Cf. *Eth. II, xx.*   [5] See *Eth. II, xxxix, Cor. et Sch.*

inadequate in the same degree, since by it the inadequacy of the original idea may be laid bare. Where this is so the two ideas remain distinct, not in respect of actuality, but of modality of self-appraisement. And knowledge of the inadequacy of a primary idea cannot utterly destroy it—not even if it is thus known to be false (though such an idea becomes, not an error, but a fiction).[1] An idea reflexively recognized as 'evident', doubtful, or fictitious maintains its place in the scale of knowing, though subordinate and, it may be, parasitical. For example, as Spinoza says, we continue to perceive the sun as relatively near even when we know it to be far distant.'[2]

Thus, with *inadequate* ideas, the 'idea' and the *idea ideae* may be distinct, not as modes of distinct Attributes, but as a more or less *critical* self-consciousness: whereas with *adequate* ideas no such distinction can be maintained; 'Certainty is nothing but the objective essence itself. . . . There is need of no other mark of the certainty of truth than the possession of a true idea. . . . Certainty and objective essence are one.'[3] And the business of philosophical method is not to eradicate what is, indeed, in-eradicable by reason of man's finite status, viz. inadequate ideas, whether 'evident', doubtful, false, or fictitious, but so to lay bare their nature and inadequacy, and its sources, as to open the way to the 'emendation of the intellect', and the moderation of the excessive power usurped by uncriticized ideas in the durational life of man.

[1] See below, pp. 86–7, 90.   [2] *Eth. II, xxxv, Sch; IV, i. et Sch.*
[3] *Tract. de Intell. Emend.*, § 35.

CHAPTER VI

THE KINDS OF KNOWLEDGE

If the *Short Treatise on God, Man, and His Wellbeing* may be taken as coming from Spinoza's own pen, and not that of a close disciple, we have three more or less variant statements by him concerning the scale of human knowing: that of the first two chapters of the second part of that work; that of the *Tractatus de Intellectus Emendatione*;[1] and that of the *Ethics*, formulated in a *Scholium* to *Proposition xl* of *Part II*, but elaborated in succeeding Propositions and Parts. These three accounts agree in distinguishing three (or four if the first is divided) more or less satisfactory kinds of knowledge: in the *Short Treatise* named Opinion or mere Belief (*Waan*), true Belief (*Geloof*), and Knowledge proper (*Weeten*); in the *Tractatus de Intellectus Emendatione*, Hearsay (*ex auditu*), Vagrant Experience (*ab experientia vaga* —a Baconian phrase), Inference from something else (*ex alia concluditur*), and Knowledge of Essence (through itself or its proximate cause); and, finally, in the *Ethics*, *Imaginatio* (or Opinion), (including knowledge from vagrant experience and from signs), *Ratio*, and *Scientia Intuitiva*. These he is wont to refer to as Knowledge of the First, Second, and Third Kinds.

The plain relation of these statements is underlined by the addition to each of the same illustration, viz. the finding of the fourth proportional to three numbers, which may either be founded, though insecurely, on a mere rule (derived either from noting the particular relations of very simple numbers, or from a schoolmaster), or again derived by calculation from the demonstrated truth of *Proposition xix* of the seventh book of Euclid's *Elements*, or, lastly, possessed by direct intuition, without calculation, of the 'adequate proportionality of the numbers'.

It is mainly with respect to the intermediate species, viz. True Belief, Inference from something else, or *Ratio*, that the accounts appear to differ according as its relation to the first or the third is prominent; and we must, of course, regard the statement in the

[1] Chs. IV and V, §§ 18–29 in Bruder's division of the work.

Ethics as the most mature and authoritative, as it is also the most closely integrated with the metaphysical system as a whole. Let us consider, then, the three kinds of knowledge *seriatim*.

I. *IMAGINATIO*, OPINION, OR THE FIRST KIND OF KNOWLEDGE

That the term '*Imaginatio*' refers to the conditions commonly supposed to govern the processes of sense-perception is clearly stated by Spinoza in *Ethices II, xvii, Sch.*: Peter's idea of Paul 'manifests the essence of Peter's body' rather than that of Paul's. The changes in Peter's body by reason of the presence of that of Paul are called 'images' of Paul in Peter 'in order to retain the customary phraseology', though it must not be supposed that they in any way *resemble* Paul. Thus, when Peter perceives Paul by the means of such 'images' he is said to 'imagine' Paul. The alternative term 'opinion' evidently derives chiefly from the first form of this kind of knowledge, viz. hearsay or mere information.

But it must not be supposed that this kind of knowledge is confined to the naïve *data* of uncriticized experience. We are informed, of course, of matters that we could not have experienced directly, e.g. our day of birth and parentage; sense-perception itself is more or less amplified by ideational processes. 'Through vagrant experience I know that I shall die, for I affirm it because I have seen that others of the same nature as myself die. . . . I also know that oil is the proper fuel for feeding flame, and that water is apt to extinguish it . . . that the dog is a barking animal, and man a rational animal.'[1] Again, to *Imaginatio* belong all abstract universals, for they arise 'because the human body . . . can form distinctly in itself only a certain number of images. . . . If this number be exceeded the images will become confused'.[2] Abstract universals are thus 'ideas in the highest degree confused' and 'are not formed by all men in the same way'. And so derived, they lack, and are incapable of, definition. When we set out to form definitions from which properties can be deduced our procedure must be essentially different, though *suggestions* may be gleaned from vagrant experience as to the common essences of singular things from which properties may be deduced. But the defined essence is no imaginational *abstractum*, but a *conceptum* with (as we may

---

[1] *Tract. de Intell. Emend.*, § 20. [2] *Eth. II, xl, Sch. i.*

say) 'a will of its own', capable in its measure of generating its own properties. It is no abstract species,[1] but a concrete potency-in-act, primordial or, more generally, involving its proximate cause. The deduction of properties is thus intrinsic and genetic, not extrinsic and 'linear'.

Empiricistic procedure from the presumed *data* of *Imaginatio* tends to conceal this essential change of method by regarding defined concepts as the product of inductive generalization, so that empiricistic 'science' is rather the product of the sophistication of *Imaginatio* than of true rational emendation of its distorted and debilitated projections of things. Hence arise its antinomies, paradoxes, doubts, fictions and errors, which common sense avoids by resting content with vagrant experience confined to the naïvely effluent durational *data* sophisticated only in a degree congruent with the self-limitations of finite self-reference. But once these imaginational objects are recognized as being, not *data*, but *problemata*, true science is seen to be attainable, not by more and more complex rationalization of the essentially unintelligible, but only by discovery of the sources of *Imaginatio*, and the emendation of the understanding to rational or intuitional cognition.

That *Imaginatio* is at best capable only of providing suggestions for rational science is noted by Spinoza in a footnote to § 21 of the *Tractatus*: 'When we clearly perceive that we are sensible of a particular body and no other, then we clearly deduce, I say, from that perception that our mind is united to that body, and that this union is the cause of that sensation'[2]—so runs the text, and he adds the footnote: 'Such a conclusion, although it may be certain, is nevertheless not sufficiently safe, unless great precautions are taken. For unless we take great care we immediately fall into errors, inasmuch as when we conceive things thus abstractly, and not through their true essence, they are at once confounded by the imagination. For that which in itself is one we imagine to be multiplex, and to those things that

---

[1] Even the more or less nominal definitions of abstract species prominent in Aristotelian science must possess sufficient generative power to set the subject before the mind, though they are powerless to generate their own properties save as operating (as Joachim insists) within a 'significant whole'. The properties of the Euclidean 'triangle', e.g., bear reference to the Euclidean axioms and postulates.

[2] See below, p. 89, note. 4.

we conceive abstractly, separately, and confusedly, we apply the names which are used to distinguish familiar things. Whence the former come to be imagined in the same way as we are wont to imagine the things to which the names were first applied.' A notable example[1] of the errors to which *Imaginatio* leads under rational (i.e. sophistical) treatment is the manner in which even intelligent men are accustomed to conceive the 'seeing eye' as a visual *object*—confusing the *functioning* eye (as it is in the act of seeing) with the *objective* eye (as it may be seen by another percipient, or in a mirror). They thus either misinterpret the union of 'eye' and 'seeing' (i.e. body and mind) as that of object-ive organ and 'Cartesian' soul, or, more sceptically, make of 'seeing' a quality, attribute, or disposition of the objective eye. Hence the so-called 'problem of perception'—sophistical, and thus insoluble.

II. *RATIO*, INTELLECTION, OR THE SECOND KIND OF KNOWLEDGE

I have said that a certain disharmony is evident between the accounts of *Ratio* given by Spinoza in the various treatises. In the *Tractatus* it seems to be represented as concerned with in-ferences from imaginational sources which we may broadly dis-tinguish as 'inductive' and 'deductive reasoning'. It is defined as knowledge of a thing derived from the knowledge of something else, 'but not adequately'.[2] This may take the form of an infer-ence from some effect to its cause, or again of the application of a general rule to some particular case. The first is exemplified by the inference that the mind is united with the body from the per-ception that we are sensible only of that one body; the second by the inference that the sun is greater than it looks from know-ledge that with sight one and the same thing appears as greater or less as its distance is decreased or increased.[3] As we have seen, such inferences may be 'evident' but are certainly not 'adequate'—in the one case, we infer only *some sort of union* of mind and body, but understand nothing about its nature; in the other case, no advance is made in true knowledge of the imaginational experience of the particular property of sight that is applied.

---

[1] Not culled from Spinoza. [2] §§ 19, 21. [3] § 21.

In some respects the account of 'true belief' in the *Short Treatise* seems nearer to that of *Ratio* in the *Ethics* than to this account in the *Tractatus*, though this may be due to the sketchy nature of the earliest statement. All agree in insisting upon the *truth* of the second kind of knowledge, but the *Tractatus* emphasizes its 'inadequacy' (i.e. its failure to advance *understanding*, and its *insecurity* by reason of its imaginational premisses), whereas the *Ethics* claims that, though it is not knowledge of individuals, it is *adequate* knowledge of the 'common properties' of individuals, in which all, in their degrees, participate.

It would seem, then, that Spinoza distinguishes two applications or species of intellection according as it is concerned with imaginational objects or with true *entia rationis*. In both cases it is formally valid, but as applied to *entia imaginationis* it sophisticates, not advances, understanding, whereas it is the very root of understanding as applied to the properties which are common to all individuals,[1] and of human understanding as applied to the properties which man shares with other beings in nature.[2]

According to the *Ethics*, then, *Ratio* or the Second Kind of Knowledge is apprehension of the common essence and properties of man and nature. In relation to what the human body has in common with its complement in nature the confusions and distortions of *Imaginatio* are excluded. In so far as Peter's body is in agreement with that of Paul, his *affectiones* register that agreement, and his idea of Paul is so far adequate. In apprehending his own properties he apprehends the properties of Paul in so far as they are common to both. Confusion and distortion arise from the alienation of Peter and Paul that issues from the unilateral self-reference of Peter; and this is a function of the finite status of Peter in nature. If this alienation were complete, all knowledge of Paul by Peter would be excluded; but this could only occur if Peter were of the very lowest grade of finite perfection—indeed if he were *non-ens*. Finite self-reference alienates the other in inverse proportion to the elevation of the self in the hierarchy of nature. Thus, with man conceived as belonging to the middle reaches of finite being, there remains, even under self-reference, a range of adequacy in apprehension of the other, and in this degree his other remains in community with him. This is in principle true throughout all ranges of being—for that which is

---

[1] *Eth. II, xxxviii.*   [2] *Eth. II, xxxix.*

absolutely other cannot be said even to be 'other', or indeed to 'be'.[1] *Ratio* is the apprehension of the common essences of things, and the properties which they generate; the confused and distorted *differentiae* congruent with individual eccentricity under unilateral self-reference are imaginational, and thus inadequate even when they are 'factual' or 'evident', and are thus subject to error, doubt, and fancy. 'Knowledge of the first kind is the sole cause of error, while knowledge of the second . . . kind is necessarily true.'[2]

It may be objected that since the objects of *Ratio* are but *entia rationis*, and thus do not exist, *Ratio* is not rightly called 'knowledge'. 'That which is common to all things, and is equally in the part and in the whole, forms the essence of no singular thing'[3]— yet it is 'proper' to singular things, i.e. truly belongs to them. In *Natura naturata* the whole singular essence of each finite singular is an integration of such common properties; but under unilateral finite self-reference the complement of the finite self is partially alienated, and the self itself degraded to partial community and partial confused and distorted differentiation in the degree of its finiteness—yet with a power of self-correction concomitant with its range of indefectible essence and durationally realized emendation.

Further factors operative in the Second Kind of Knowledge are hinted at by Spinoza, such as certain axioms and secondary notions,[4] but the discussion of these is 'set apart for another treatise' which does not appear to have been written, or (if we suppose that the *Tractatus de Intellectus Emendatione* is referred to—as perhaps we may) completed. Nor is the misapplication of rational processes and principles to the objects of *Imaginatio* (which I have called 'sophistication') adequately considered in either treatise, though the footnotes in the *Treatise*, to which I have referred, indicate Spinoza's awareness of problems which have become increasingly vital with the development of empiricist philosophy.

---

[1] Morality, as we shall see, is the effort to correct the otherness of the other by passage from self-reference to reference to God, i.e. to realize the perfect community characteristic of eternal creation.

[2] *Eth. II, xli.*   [3] *Eth. II, xxxvii.*   [4] *Eth. II, xl, Sch. i.*

III. *SCIENTIA INTUITIVA*, 'INTELLECTUAL LOVE', OR THE THIRD KIND OF KNOWLEDGE

According to the *Short Treatise* the clearest knowledge of all depends neither on hearsay, nor experience, nor the art of reasoning, but on 'penetration';[1] it comes 'not from our being convinced by reasons, but from our feeling and enjoying the thing itself'.[2]

The *Tractatus de Intellectus Emendatione* defines this kind of knowledge as that 'which arises when a thing is perceived through its essence alone, or through the knowledge of its proximate cause',[3] i.e. when its concept is self-generating, or generated by immanent potency. Again, 'it grasps the adequate essence of the thing without danger of error'.[4] Thus, by actually knowing anything, I understand what it is to know[5] (so that the *idea ideae*, i.e. the idea of the mind itself, is necessarily so far 'intuitive') e.g. knowledge of the nature of the mind involves knowledge that it is united with the body.[6]

The formal definition of *Scientia Intuitiva* given in the *Ethics* is often quoted, but rarely understood and explained by expositors: 'This kind of knowing proceeds from an adequate idea of the formal essence of certain Attributes of God to the adequate knowledge of the essence of things.'[7] And it must be allowed that to the contemporary mind, steeped in empiricistic presuppositions, it is exceedingly laconic. Its obscurity, however, stems from the general failure to understand Spinoza's doctrine of the essential nature of the adequate idea as the intrinsically generative concept. So long, e.g. as 'adequacy' is identified with mere intrinsic coherence of 'ideal content', and 'truth' with its correspondence with an extrinsic thing, the distinction of *Ratio* and *Scientia Intuitiva* must appear either unimportant or incomprehensible: unimportant because coherence is equally characteristic of *Ratio*; incomprehensible if in *Scientia Intuitiva* the mind 'feels and enjoys the thing itself'. To the idealist, rejecting correspondence of idea and thing as defining truth, the distinction fades to complete unimportance. Thus we find Joachim looking beyond epistemology for the basis of the distinction: 'Spinoza's conception of "scientia intuitiva" is unintelligible

---

[1] II, i.   [2] II, ii.   [3] § 19.   [4] § 29.   [5] § 22.   [6] *Loc. cit.*
[7] *Eth. II, xl, Sch. ii.*

apart from his conception of the "Freedom", "Happiness", or "Salvation" of man, i.e. man's attainment of the practical ideal.'[1] But though it is true enough that *Scientia Intuitiva* is closely related to human wellbeing, there is no reason to think that it is unintelligible epistemologically. Even further from the truth are those who suppose that in this region of his speculation Spinoza is a mystic rather than a philosopher. The difficulties which have driven many to such expedients in the exposition of Spinoza's thought arise chiefly from taking imaginational knowledge as exemplary in form, and seeking to interpret the Third Kind of Knowledge in terms of this *exemplar*, whereas for Spinoza it is *Scientia Intuitiva* that is knowledge *par excellence*, of which *Imaginatio* and *Ratio* are, respectively, distorted and abstract expressions. Thus, if we approach the subject of knowledge (as Descartes would say) 'analytically', *Scientia intuitiva* is knowledge purged from the special confusions and distortions of *Imaginatio*, and from the special limitations of *Ratio* the objects of which are not singulars, not *entia realia*, but *entia rationis*;[2] and if we proceed 'synthetically', *Ratio* and *Imaginatio* must be understood as forms of knowledge under, respectively, dissection by reason of human limitation and distortion by reason of self-reference.

Scientia intuitiva is knowledge at once adequate and individual, having both the 'intrinsic' and the 'extrinsic denominations'[3] of the true idea in its proper excellence. To understand its nature, therefore, it is necessary to understand the nature and properties of the action of knowing as such.

To *know* and mentally to *be*, we have seen, are one and the same. The mind does not 'have' ideas—it *is* an idea more or less complex and integral. Mind is knowing agency in act. But cognition implies a *cognitum* which must primarily be something extrinsic. For to know itself as knowing agent, i.e. to exist as *cognitum*, it must first of all know something other than itself. With the human mind this something extrinsic is the human body, with which, therefore, it is in this way united. And as the *Tractatus* suggests, all human knowledge is to this extent 'intuitive',

---

[1] *A Study of the Ethics of Spinoza*, p. 181.
[2] 'That which is common to all, and is equally in the part and in the whole, forms the essence of no individual being' (*Eth. II, xxxvii*).
[3] *Eth. II, Def. iv, et Explic.*

since whenever I know anything I understand intuitively, among other things, that, as knowing, the mind is united with the body.[1]

Further, every finite individual body, or physical agent, exists and is constituted by its active relations with its complement in physical nature. Even the imaginational body is 'affected' by extrinsic bodies, and the real body as it is in itself, i.e. as created or as referred to God, is constituted by participation in properties common to itself and its complement in *Natura naturata*. It is in virtue of the clear and undistorted relations of the agency of the self and that of its complement under *Scientia Intuitiva* that this form of knowledge is more excellent than *Imaginatio*; and in virtue of its integrity that it is more excellent than *Ratio*.

Now, it is this community of the parts in the whole, i.e. of the microcosms in the macrocosm as all actualize the primordial potency-in-act, that Spinoza regards as the essence of love; which, as enjoyed by emended mind is 'Intellectual Love'. It is true that he speaks of 'the intellectual love of God which *arises from* the third kind of knowledge',[2] but this is but a methodological supposition. There is no passage from perfect knowledge to intellectual love as there may be with durational learning a passage which is 'joy' and is associated with the idea of an object to constitute 'imaginational love';[3] 'if joy consists in the passage to a greater perfection, blessedness' (which is 'nothing but the tranquillity of mind which springs from the intuitive knowledge of God')[4] 'must indeed consist in this, that the mind is endowed with perfection itself'.[5] The intellectual love of God, we might say, is the 'idea of the intuitive idea', which, as we know, is identical with the idea itself.

With these principles in mind—viz. that in all knowledge there is involved awareness of self as cognitive agent united with a primary *cognitum* other than mental (and with the human mind physical); that this *cognitum* cannot be wholly isolated from a complement of like beings, but exists by relation with them, durationally or eternally; and that knowledge is perfect in so far as it takes the form of 'intellectual love' by the realization of the constitutive community of self and congruent complement (imaginationally obscured and distorted to the form of confused

---

[1] *Tract. de Intell. Emend.*, § 22.   [2] *Eth. V, xxxiii.*   [3] *Eth. V, xxxiii, Sch.*
[4] *Eth. IV, Append. iv.*   [5] *Eth. V, xxxiii, Sch.*

affectio, and rationally truncated to that of partial community of property)—we can understand that the human mind, in so far as its knowledge is perfect in kind, is the idea of physical Nature *qua* manifested in, and constituting, the human body as it is united with itself, i.e. with a mind that finitely manifests Nature as mental. Thus, to have 'intuitive knowledge' of anything is to possess its nature as a manifestation of Nature, and to enjoy this possession as a mind manifesting the mind of Nature. And since Nature itself (i.e. *Natura naturata*) is, in the human perspective, the actuality of certain Attributes of God, viz. Thought and Extension (i.e. the primordial potency-in-act as 'determining the intellect'), it follows that 'this kind of knowing proceeds from an adequate idea of the formal essence of certain Attributes of God, to the adequate knowledge of the essence of things'. Thus, Spinoza does not (as many have supposed to be necessary) confine *Scientia Intuitiva* to the 'mind of God' enjoying itself as identical with non-mental Nature, but assigns it also to the human mind—and as no mere ideal, but as both fundamental in psychophysical self-knowledge, and indefinitely attainable by self-emendation in the knowledge of God and 'things'.

Finally, something must be said on the question raised by Joachim and others, whether, and if so in what way, *Scientia Intuitiva* involves rational inference of the kind assigned to the Second Kind of Knowledge. According to Joachim 'there is an inference in "scientia intuitiva": but the inference is immanent and absorbed in the final intuition', whereas 'in "ratio", the inference remains external to the conclusion, and the knowledge of the conclusion remains therefore discursive'; 'the discursive movement remains within the whole' which is given.[1] Others have noted that Spinoza's own definition of *Scientia Intuitiva* stresses its inferential nature, since it speaks of a process from one adequate idea to another.

I will not stay here to comment on Joachim's suggestion in the passage quoted that in discursive inference the conclusion remains external to the inference, save to note its paradoxical nature. It will be more profitable to recall that, according to the *Tractatus*, *Ratio* is the knowledge of a thing which arises when its essence is deduced from something else, but not adequately[2]—

---

[1] *A Study of the Ethics of Spinoza*, p. 184.
[2] *Tract. de Intell. Emend.*, § 19.

'not adequately' meaning that what is deduced is a mere 'that', and not an adequate 'what', 'how', or 'why' (e.g. *that* mind and body are united, but not *how* they are united; *that* the sun is greater than it looks, but not *why* it should be so). Again, in the *Ethics*, *Ratio* is described as knowledge of things through their 'common properties'—such knowledge being, though adequate so far as it goes, unable to probe to the singularity of things, its objects being *entia rationis* and not *entia realia*. By *Ratio* we have knowledge of Peter *qua* 'man', but not of Peter *qua* Peter. The inferences of *Ratio*, therefore, though certain, are truncated by reason of their generality, and no individual essence can by their means be concluded. Or rather, perhaps we should say, between what is true of Peter *qua* man, and the true essence of Peter, there remains a gap only capable of being filled by an infinity of such inferences. But knowledge *par excellence* is of the real, i.e. of the individual. Such knowledge is enjoyed by the individual man in the very act of knowing anything, however imperfectly, seeing that, as Descartes claimed, in that act he intuits his own active being. Thus *Imaginatio* itself is rooted in intuition, though by reason of its unwitting eccentricity of projection under finite self-reference, the individuals ostensibly perceived exhibit their real natures as greatly confused, fragmented, divided and contorted.[1] Under *Ratio* their incorrigible factors are distilled, but at the cost of their finite individuality; and it is only in so far as the mind, as epistemically united with the body, is thereby, by way of mutual adaptation, or love, able to 'feel and enjoy the thing itself', as with the mind itself united with the body, it expresses, according to its grade of perfection, the primordial potency-in-act. Here inference is no mere resolution of an implication, no movement from the idea of one thing to that of another through community of selected property, but the actualization of the primordial potency-in-act in so far as it is the *fons et origo* of the thing—or, where the thing so apprehended is remote from its original source, through the immanent mediation of its proximate cause taken as the immediate vehicle of that potency. And this is possible only in so far as the mind refers all things, or those immediately relevant, to God. For thus only is

---

[1] 'Greatly', but not wholly: for there is no *pure Imaginatio*, any more than there can be *pure Ratio*; and each is suffused by the immanent power of self-emendation.

the eternal stream of creation apprehended without distortion, and without abstraction.

Ratio rests upon *selective* community of property, but perfect knowledge demands the communization of *all* the properties of the knower and the known by the transformation of the differentiating *affectiones* of *Imaginatio* into the mutual responsiveness of agents distinct by reason of their mutual adaptation. *For though the identity of 'things' excludes their distinction, that of 'agents' is its very foundation.*

G

CHAPTER VII

INADEQUATE KNOWLEDGE

The extreme simplicity of the principles governing adequate knowledge—knowledge properly so called—is in direct contrast with the complexity of the conditions governing inadequate knowledge—what Joachim has called 'pseudo-cognizance'. This complication has its source in the confusion and distortion of the mind's objects under its unilateral finite self-reference. Human knowledge merits the name of 'knowledge' though it is subject to limitation in amplitude (as confined to the Attributes of Thought and Extension) and to varying degrees of obfuscation by which it fades off from the perfection of form of which it is capable to a *nimbus* of *Imaginatio* in which that form is distorted, and its objects confused and dissipated, by reason of self-reference—a *nimbus* indefinitely focalizable under rational principle. Here we are concerned with the nature, cognitive status, and truth-value of the factors constituting this *penumbra* of *Imaginatio*.

First, it must be noted that the unilateral self-reference of the finite individual must not be conceived as in itself vicious, and thus without defence and void. *Imaginatio* is not the same thing as illusion or ignorance. For the finite agent as a microcosmic individual *is* a 'self' upon the 'axes' of which its macrocosmic complement can be projected, and through the 'screen' of which that complement is riddled. Its objects are distorted, confused, and depleted—not veiled and utterly hidden. The most inadequate of ideas is still an 'idea' with some kind of object, and not a form of ignorance.

This is most obviously true where the imaginational idea is the unsophisticated apprehension of the *affectiones* of the body, i.e. of the screened and distorted projections of the parts of its complement with respect to itself. Such imaginations are 'not opposed to truth, nor do they disappear with the presence of the truth'. They disappear only when 'other imaginations arise which are stronger, and which exclude the present existence of the objects we imagine'.[1]

---

[1] *Eth. IV, i, Sch.* This, of course, is true of *all* imaginations.

Such ineliminable imaginations I shall venture to call 'evident' or 'factual' ideas, to distinguish them, on the one hand, from the 'authentic' or self-generating ideas of *Ratio* and *Scientia Intuitiva*, and on the other, from those imaginational ideas which are false, dubious, fanciful, suppositious, or hypothetical, the objects of which are more obscure.

I. THE 'EVIDENT' OR 'FACTUAL' IDEA

Both the inadequacy and the 'evidence' of the 'factual' idea stem from man's inclusion in Nature—in virtue of which inclusion the assumption of the attitude of interested extrinsic spectator of the world is defensible only because, and in so far as, that 'world' is not the Nature in which man's body is embedded, nor an adequate expression of it, but the more or less distorted and abstracted projection of the body's complement in Nature as referred to the body which is but a 'part' of Nature more or less fully and adequately expressing the 'whole'. Such imaginational apprehension need thus neither be false nor an ignorant illusion of knowledge—though it certainly falls short of ideal authenticity or self-generative certainty. In this perspective the individuality of Nature and its 'parts' is fragmented, and its eternity telescoped-out to duration; but it is not destroyed. Furthermore, self-referent ideas which are incorrigible save by the correction of finite self-reference enjoy a positive epistemic status relative to man, in spite of their inadequacy; and in human experience maintain themselves even in the presence of truth or adequate ideas. Thus, Spinoza says: 'When we look at the sun we imagine its distance from us to be about 200 feet' (we need not cavil at the precise estimate), and 'although we may afterwards know that the sun is more than 600 diameters of the earth distant from us, we still imagine it near us . . . not because we are ignorant of its true distance, but because an *affectio* of our body involves the essence of the sun, in so far as our body itself is "affected" by it.'[1] Similarly, even when we know that 'freedom' is not action without a cause, we still *feel* free when we are unaware of the cause of our action, say in so-called 'free decision'.

Spinoza's own way of expressing this set of relations is in terms of '*affectiones*': the human mind has inadequate ideas of Nature

[1] *Eth. II, xxxv, Sch.; IV, i, Sch.*

which, though *prima facie* they appear to be ideas of independent things with which the body, similarly conceived, has relations of co-operation and strife, are really only ideas of the *affectiones* of the body as related to its complement. These 'images' of things do not 'reproduce the forms of the things', so that the ideas of them which the mind, as the idea of the body, involves are inadequate, confused, and fragmentary. What it is important to notice is that the 'images' of things do not fail to reproduce the forms of things because the body is wholly different in nature from its complement, for, rightly understood, the body and its complement are in agreement within the range of the body's finite potency; but because, by reason of self-reference, this eternal agreement is disorganized from the standpoint of the self, in proportion to its finiteness, and gives place to the strife and concession of self and other characteristic of the *affectio* as distinct from the 'common property'. Yet this is but a distinction, not a separation, for all concession so far expresses community, and all strife is parasitical on community. Things which have nothing in common cannot suffer conflict.

The depletion of eternal community to the form of durational and conative historicity is thus not its occultation but its self-referent appearance, and is involved in falsity, dubiety, and illusion only in so far as it is uncritically assigned an ontological status that it cannot claim or sustain. The deliverances of naïve experience, though not adequate, are the evidences provided under self-reference from which, by the emendation of the intellect, and of its objects, true certainty may be distilled—nature's rough hammers by the use of which well-designed hammers may be forged.[1]

This, then, is the truth that lies *perdue* in the empiricistic dogma concerning the relations of true knowledge and immediate experience; not that unemended experience provides the foundation and verificatory norm of all developed knowledge, so that the mind is anchored to its empirical *data* (whether of sense merely, or of this 'realized' by conative agency), but that from its more or less unintelligible deliverances the mind is set upon the path of emendation in the light of intellectual principles already imperfectly, privatively, and problematically actualized in them. These are the true anchors of the mind by the traction of which alone

[1] *Tract. de Intell. Emend.*, § 30.

it can ride the storms and buffetings of mere experience, the *empirically* incorrigible *data* of which are, in truth, privations of the real, and thus rather to be called '*ablata*', and by nature *metaphysically* corrigible. The 'evidence' of the 'factual idea' stems from the relation of its object to that of the adequate or authentic idea, not the truth of the theoretical or derivative idea from the 'evidence' of empirical *data*. Only a firm grasp of this principle can dissuade the mind, whatever sceptics may say, from the attempt, sooner or later, either to make of the objects of *Imaginatio* those 'real things' by which the vulgar and the natural realist[1] are so enslaved, or to seek among its objects the original ineluctable sense-*data*, purged from every intellectual gloss, which may be regarded as the objects of incorrigible apprehension, the ideas of which must be the very norms of knowledge. Thus immersed in *Imaginatio*, unwitting of its eccentricity, the mind, by its very nature even under this self-limitation, must exercise its *nisus* to clear apprehension—but now by the mere rationalization of the objects of *Imaginatio* without metaphysical transcendence: a 'rationalization' that by reason of this limitation is but sophistication when employed with a view to a knowledge of Nature and its 'parts' *in se*.[2]

II. MODES OF EVIDENTIAL DEFECT

It should now be clear that a distinction must be drawn between the *properly* true idea which is adequate or *asserts* no more than is contained or is immanent in its concept, and the 'evident' idea which is not false, doubtful, or fictitious, though it is inadequate, and which *assents* to the imaginationally incorrigible. To 'assert' and to 'assent to' are related as truth proper to 'evidence'. Thus 'evidence', involving 'assent', involves a defect of truth proper, and falsity, dubiety, and fancy involve a further defect of 'evidence'. I say 'involve' because these ideas cannot be explained as mere defects of truth or of 'evidence', for thus they would be species, not of knowledge, but of ignorance. One and all, they are *privations* of truth or 'evidence', i.e. more or less unrecognized

---

[1] In this matter there is little to choose between realists and idealists of all schools; their differences lie elsewhere.

[2] There is no need or wish here to suggest that the scientific rationalization of empirical *data* is wholly lacking in utility in the conduct of imaginational life. The peril lies in unawareness, or even denial, of its *philosophical* limitations.

defects. By reason of self-reference the 'evident' idea is apt to make an unmerited truth-claim, and by reason of fragmentariness the false idea claims an 'evidence' not rightly conceded. Again, as we shall see, the doubtful idea involves awareness of defect of 'evidence' and the suspension of assent, while the fictitious idea ignores, or for some reason resists, rejection, and against the 'evidence', intrinsic or extrinsic, maintains assent. And the false, the doubtful, and the fictitious ideas, as involving defect of 'evidence' *a fortiori* involve defect of truth proper, so that they are corrigible both on the imaginational and on the intellectual levels, i.e. by clarification or investigation, or by more fundamental 'reference to God' by which all ideas are adequated.

In short, then, *only* imaginational ideas can be false, dubious, or fictitious; *not all* of them are so characterized; and *none* of them are *properly* true. Thus we are involved in error not only when we take an imaginational idea to be properly true, but also when we take that to be 'evident' which is not. In error there is privation of truth or of 'evidence' (and therefore also of truth): in Spinoza's own words, 'falsity consists in the privation of knowledge which inadequate, i.e. mutilated and confused, ideas involve'; 'in ideas there is nothing positive in virtue of which they are said to be false' (for even 'assent' is a defect of intellectual assertion); and 'all ideas in so far as they are referred to God are true'.[1]

Further, inadequate ideas are 'mutilated and confused', and it is from this character that falsity, dubiety, and fancy emanate: for one and all they are composite and lack the genetic integrity of truth proper. Thus falsity, dubiety, and fancy are functions of the bizarre, alternative, or factitious composition of mutilated ideas. Let us consider them *seriatim*.

1. *The False Idea*

Spinoza's doctrine of error has suffered greatly from the order in which he chose, in the *Tractatus*, to consider the species of pseudo-cognizance, beginning with the fictitious idea, and passing thence to the false and the doubtful. For thus it comes to be suggested that falsity consists in superadding 'assent' to a fiction, whereas it is truer to say that fiction consists in the refusal to

---

[1] *Eth. II, xxxv; xxxiii; xxxii.*

withdraw assent from an error. The modern notion of an 'idea' as something objective to which assent, assertion, or judgement must be added, is wholly unspinozistic. The very essence of the idea is for him its mental agency, whether it takes the form of assertion, of assent, of suspension of assent, or of its suppositious maintenance. Failure to apply this principle lies at the root of Joachim's attempted destructive criticism of Spinoza's doctrine of error in the *Tractatus*, added to his failure to distinguish intellectual assertion and imaginational assent, so that he cannot understand why Spinoza treats assent 'not as a positive asset, but as a defect',[1] as involving only a 'tendency to affirm'.[2] The result is that Joachim denies that for Spinoza there can *be* a 'false idea',[3] on the ground that as false it cannot be intellectually affirmed; and asserts that what passes under that name is no more than 'a mere conjunction of terms associated in the imagination, a complex image masquerading as a genuine idea or integral act of thought'.[4] The mind, he thinks, contributes nothing to error, for the assent is not 'anything *positive* in the experience or in the attitude of the erring mind'.[5] But why should the description of assent as a defect of intellectual affirmation imply that it is 'nothing positive'? 7 is a *positive* number though it is 12 *minus* 5!

Spinoza's essential doctrine of error must not, then, be hastily gathered from his rather ill-advised preliminary statement that 'there is no difference between' the false and the fictitious ideas 'excepting that the false idea supposes assent, i.e. . . . that no causes are offered when the presentations themselves are offered by which, as with fancy, it is possible to gather that they do not arise from things beyond themselves, and that it is almost the same as dreaming with eyes open or while awake'.[6] As well might it be argued that he held that true ideas do 'arise from things beyond themselves'. Ideas are actions of the mind, and neither arise from external things, nor can be conceived as wholly lacking intrinsic agency in the form of assertion, assent, suspension, or supposition. Even the fictitious idea, *qua* idea, is no mere passive association of 'ideal contents'; and the false idea is no such chimerical entity to which assent has been superadded. In error imaginationally associated ideas that are mutilated and confused

---

[1] *Spinoza's Tractatus de Intellectus Emendatione, A Commentary*, p. 152.
[2] *Op. cit.*, pp. 152, 163.   [3] *Op. cit.*, p. 156.   [4] *Op. cit.*, p. 156.
[5] *Op. cit.*, p. 163.   [6] *Tract. de Intell. Emend.*, § 66.

are compounded, and because no causes are presented such as to exclude their integration as 'factual' (much less, certain) the compound idea involves assent. The savage lying by a tree hears a voice and sees no man, so believes that the tree spoke: the idea is false because it involves assent to the confused idea of a tree speaking, and because this confused idea cannot be 'factually' or intellectually clarified—the tree has no organs of speech, and cannot speak without them. Again, the idea that 'Peter exists' which may be in some man's mind, even though in fact Peter does exist, cannot be true in the absence of grounds: 'The thought, so far as that man is concerned is false . . . or if it be preferred so to speak, it is not true.'[1] If we say, then, that the falsity lies in the unwarranted assent (or assertion even) when mere imaginational association, by reason of the lack of countervailing ideas, or dubious composition, by reason of their insufficiency, passes as 'evidence' (or even certainty), this does not mean that to an 'ideal content' we superadd an incongruent degree of assertion. For in an 'idea' the assertion is the essence, and the supposed 'ideal content' nothing in its absence, at least, no *ens reale*. In error, by reason of imaginational mutilation and confusion, i.e. from lack of a sufficient countervailing complement, and the fragmentary nature of the associated parts, there is assertion without adequate ground, or assent without imaginational incorrigibility. Thus, though 'there is nothing positive in ideas in virtue of which they are said to be false',[2] such ideas are not forms of nescience, but of cognition—error is not ignorance, not defect of knowledge, but seeming knowledge by reason of defect. *Complete* error would *be* ignorance, but no error is complete: always it is parasitical on partial truth or 'evidence'. The agency which is the mind, lacking its proper intrinsic discipline and extrinsic guidance runs into error by reason of the defect; for to assert, or to assent, or to doubt, or to suppose, or in some way mentally to act or to endeavour, is its *sine qua non*.

2. *The Doubtful Idea*

'Doubt', says Spinoza, 'is nothing but the suspension of the mind about some affirmation or negation which we should affirm or deny unless something occurred by ignorance of which knowledge

---

[1] *Tract. de Intell. Emend.*, § 69. See above, p. 62, note 3.   [2] *Eth. II, xxxiii*.

of that thing must be imperfect.'[1] 'Doubt is caused by another idea which is not so clear and distinct that we can infer from it any certainty concerning the thing about which we doubt.'[2] Once again, this must not be interpreted as meaning that in dubiety the mind is presented with alternative 'ideal contents' about which it is unable to exercise any mental agency. Doubt is not *suspense* of judgement, for thus it would not be a mental action at all—it is the *suspension* of judgement, the *active withholding* of assent, not its mere absence, not a state of passivity.[3]

In doubt the mind suspends assent to the composition of associated ideas by reason of the operation of other ideas which, though not sufficiently 'evident' to negate the composition, conflict with it. I am in doubt whether I see Peter when I recall that he is very like Paul, and without this recollection the idea of the presence of Peter would raise no doubt: 'Doubt is never produced in the mind by the thing itself concerning which we doubt, i.e. if there be only a single idea in the mind, whether it be true or false, there is neither doubt nor certainty, but only a certain act of apprehension (*sensatio*), for the idea is in itself nothing but this act of apprehension.'[4] In adequate cognition there is no possibility either of error or of dubiety, for such an idea substantiates itself, and what is opposed to it must be rejected. The same must be true of ideas *genuinely* 'evident', save in so far as they are taken to be *metaphysically incorrigible* (for then they are subject to dubitation by the presence of adequate ideas). Such ideas, being imaginationally incorrigible, constitute metaphysical *problemata* under the opposition of self-substantiating adequate ideas, and thus promote metaphysical speculation, i.e. inquiry into their sources. Doubt arises within the sphere of *Imaginatio*, naïve or rationalized (i.e. sophisticated), and may concern either 'facts' or theories. So-called 'rational doubts' are not doubts concerning reason, but concerning the employment of reason within a sphere

[1] *Tract. de Intell. Emend.*, § 80.   [2] *Op. cit.*, § 78.

[3] Joachim thinks that a statement of *Eth. II, xlix, Sch.*, where Spinoza is arguing that suspending judgement is not an act of free decision, makes of it '*nothing but* awareness of partial ignorance' (*Commentary*, p. 197)—no sort of action of the mind, but its complete absence. This is typical of Joachim's 'Eleatic' approach to Spinoza's doctrine of inadequate knowledge, which is thus made to 'fall hopelessly to pieces'.

[4] Not 'sensation' in the modern sense. *Sensatio* is a noun of action, clearly related to the notion of 'assent'.

that by its very nature and origin is subject only to a sophistical reason, or subject to *Ratio* only by emendation.

We need not linger on the subject of the doubtful idea: all who have grasped Spinoza's account of error will have little difficulty in understanding that of doubt, and that little will be sufficiently met under the next head, viz. the fictitious idea, where the same principles are carried to a further issue.

3. *The Fictitious Idea*

The notion of fiction as the mere passage of 'floating ideal contents' which in error the mind assents to without 'evidence', is one that, as I have said, Spinoza's own order of consideration in the *Tractatus* tends to encourage in the already biased modern mind, but which must be firmly rejected. It is, indeed, excluded by the doctrine of the *Tractatus* itself, so far at least as supposals (which occupy most of the ground) are said to be actual or possible errors recognized as errors but nevertheless in certain circumstances maintained in that form without correction.[1] I can suppose that the world is flat because, though I know that it is a globe, it is possible to fall into error by reason of appearances. Such a fiction is thus an idea that might involve erroneous assent, so that what is either impossible or necessary cannot be subject to fancy. Now, the recognition of the falsity of an idea is an act of the mind, and not the mere collapse of the idea. It is thus that the detected falsity can be maintained as a supposal, the assent being thus modified by reduction to the form of fancy involving its own form of mental action, and not the passivity of nescience.

Not all fictitious ideas, however, are supposals: there is 'mere fancy' or reverie which is not much discussed by Spinoza in the *Tractatus*. 'A fancy considered in itself,' he says, 'does not differ much from a dream, save that in dreams causes are not offered which, by the aid of the senses, are presented to those awake, from which they gather that those presentations are not, at that time, presented by things placed outside of them.'[2] Here we have described the fictitious idea in its most naïve form, in which the recognition of error which distinguishes a supposal is absent, inchoate, or undiscriminated. Or perhaps we may regard it as a condition or factor present throughout the whole range of

[1] § 56.   [2] § 64, note.

fictitious ideas, and more or less prominent. Though in that case they cannot be rigorously separated, it may be well to consider these types of fictitious idea separately.

a. *Fancy*

It is mere fancy or reverie that is most liable to be taken to be 'floating ideal content' with the mind wholly passive, merely attending involuntarily to phantasmal objects. Spinoza could, of course, admit no such account of reverie, for an 'idea' is an *action* of the mind, and where there is no action there can be no idea. What sort of mental action, then, is mere fancying? This is a topic on which the views of Spinoza must be collected, for his account of the fictitious idea in the *Tractatus* is mainly concerned with supposals. Most pertinent, perhaps, are some remarks that he interposes 'by the way' in § 55, in which he notes that both the essence and the existence of any thing may be conceived either more generally or more particularly: 'the more generally existence is conceived the more confusedly it is conceived, and the more easily it can be assigned to any given thing; on the other hand, when it is more particularly conceived it is more clearly understood, and it is ascribed with more difficulty to any thing, except to the thing by itself when we do not attend to the order of nature'. Now in mere fancy or reverie plainly we are not attending to the order of nature, but allowing to our ideas unlicensed scope. It is not that the mind is inactive, but that it is undisciplined.

Here we may note also a remark in a note to § 57: 'imagination never creates, nor offers to the mind, any new thing, but . . . those things only which are in the brain, or in the imagination, are awakened in the memory, and . . . the mind confusedly occupies itself with them all simultaneously. For example, speech and a tree are remembered, and the mind confusedly attending to them thinks that the tree speaks.' The elements of the composite idea of fancy are thus in some sense not fanciful at all, but involve assent: each is a '*sensatio*' or act of apprehension.[1] Now reverie involves the more or less undisciplined composition of such *sensationes* without due attention to the order of nature, or even to their intrinsic coherence. I say 'without *due* attention' for fancy is not wholly undisciplined. We can fancy a fly indefinitely

[1] See above, p. 89, note 4.

larger than any we have ever seen, but not an infinite fly; that Adam had wings, but not that his body lacked extent; that a tree speaks, but not that its colour is audible—though certainly we can conjoin the words. For an infinite fly could have no external conformation; human bodies are by nature extended; and colour is a visual, not auditory, quality. The compositions of fancy exclude patent impossibilities, though by reason of inattention to the order of nature, and the vague general conceptions of the elements compounded, i.e. fragmentariness and confusion, factitious bizarreries are tolerated, with only a vague sense of their hypernatural status.

Thus in mere fancy or reverie assent is not lacking with respect to the elements or their composition, but it is more or less undisciplined by attention to the order of nature intrinsic and extrinsic to the elements compounded—'attention' being the actuality of the actual idea.

b. *Supposal*

In supposal, the general nature of which has already been indicated, such discipline is not merely lacking, but is privative. What is known, more or less generally, to be erroneous is maintained experimentally—not *assented* to, but *supposed*. And we suppose, not in order positively to enlarge our knowledge of nature, but in order either to particularize the exact point of our generally conceived error, or, perhaps, to convict another of error, or again to win some practical advantage over him. Thus, we may suppose a candle burning in a vacuum in order to understand, or to exhibit, exactly why (as we know in general that it does not) it cannot do so. We suppose that a proposition is false in order to show by *reductio ad absurdum* that it is true. We suppose a man to live a thousand years in order to discredit the supposed benefits of immortality. The dishonest trader supposes that his customer is ignorant in order to sell an inferior article.

Here, then, even less than in mere fancy, the total exclusion of mental agency is incredible, though the agency takes neither the form of the assertion of the certain, nor that of assent to the 'evident', nor that of the suspension of assent. Supposition is a composite idea involving experimental assent to what is more or less generally understood to the supposer to be false—or at least, we must add, dubious.

III. HYPOTHESIS AND FREE IMAGINATION

In some of his writings, it must also be noticed, Spinoza makes what may well be regarded as a further extension of the conception of a fictitious idea. This has been generally overlooked, but is of great importance. In *Part III* of his *Geometrical Version of Descartes's Principles of Philosophy* he discusses the epistemological status of hypotheses such as that of Descartes about the generation of the 'visible universe' from the movements of the original angular particles of matter or extension. Such an hypothesis, to be valid, must involve no contradictions, and be capable of providing the bases of deduction of what is observed in nature; and to be worth elaborating must be the simplest possible, and easy to grasp. But what of its *truth*? It is not at all necessary for this, he says, that the world should actually have been generated in this way—indeed, we know very well that it was not. Nevertheless, the hypothesis may be a satisfactory exposition of the nature of things, far better than any description of their nature as they now are could be. He gives an example: 'If anyone should find drawn on a sheet of paper the curved line which we call a parabola, and should wish to investigate its nature, it is all one whether he supposed the line to be first cut from some cone, and thence impressed on the paper, or whether he supposed it to be described by the motion of two straight lines, or to have arisen in some other way, provided that from what he supposes he shall demonstrate all the properties of the parabola. . . . Thus also, to explicate the lineaments of nature it is permissible for us freely to assume any hypothesis if only from it we may deduce all the phenomena of nature by mathematical inferences.' Thus true knowledge of the world may be embodied in a fictional account of its genesis and history—a fiction that differs from the truth only, as he says, in the order in which the forms of things appear. And in that case, 'there is no fear of error from a false hypothesis'.[1]

Since the treatise from which I have quoted is Cartesian in content, it is of interest to note a more or less parallel expression

---

[1] Similarly, it might be suggested, particle or wave-theory hypotheses of the structure of matter may be fictional, and yet embody truth—the real constituents of nature being quite other, though their laws of action may be thus expressed.

which is unexceptionably spinozistic, viz. that of *free imagination*:
'the mind is not in error because it imagines . . . if the mind,
when it imagines non-existent things to be present, could at the
same time know that those things did not really exist, it would
attribute this power of imagining to a virtue and not a fault of its
nature, especially if this faculty of imagining depended on its own
nature alone, i.e. if this mental faculty of imagining were free'.[1]
It is to the *Tractatus Theologico-Politicus* that we must look for
the most notable example of what Spinoza here intends. 'The
prophets were endowed with unusually vivid imaginations, and
not with unusually perfect minds. . . . Men of great imaginational
power are less fitted for abstract reasoning, whereas those that
excel in intellect and its use keep their imagination more restrained and controlled, holding it in subjection, so to speak, lest
it should usurp the place of reason.'[2] Now the prophets imagined
God as an external law-giver, and his laws as the decrees of a
monarch—a conception that is fictional; nevertheless, the import
of their message though presented, from the philosophical standpoint, in fictitious form, is morally 'evident' in so far as it sets
forth true moral principles adapted to the intelligence of the multitude, and thus tends to further 'piety' among men. The imaginations of the prophets about the nature and dispositions of
God, the manner in which he is 'the *exemplar* of the true life',
how he is omnipresent and freely directs all things, rewards the
good and punishes the evil, and so on, were fictitious; but through
these fictions much true moral doctrine was promulgated, and
obedience thereto quickened. Speculatively the prophetic imagination was in bondage, but morally it was free; and 'faith does not
so much require truth as piety. . . . The best faith is not necessarily possessed by him who displays the best reasons, but by
him who displays the best fruits of justice and charity.'[3] How
these intellectual and ethical principles are to be reconciled under
the metaphysical principles of Spinoza has still to be made clear
in the chapters which follow; here we are concerned only with the
value which may reside in, or be conveyed by, ideas which are
speculatively fictitious. For what is true of philosophy and faith
may well also be true of philosophy and art, of philosophy and
natural science, of philosophy and technology, of philosophy and

[1] *Eth. II, xvii, Sch.*   [2] *Tract. Theo.-Pol.*, ch. 2.
[3] *Op. cit.*, ch. 14.

common sense—that in so far as what is essential to art, to natural science, to technology, or to common sense, may well be conveyed by, or reside in, ideas which speculatively are fictitious, and which, if assented to as speculatively true or 'evident', are plainly false.

CHAPTER VIII

THE *AFFECTUS* AND MENTAL DISPOSITIONS

Most writers on what may broadly be called Spinoza's 'psychology' have experienced difficulty in providing a suitable equivalent in modern English for his term '*affectus*', and many have had recourse to the term 'emotion'. Joachim, who does so, wishes to use this term 'as roughly equivalent to the German "*Stimmung*"', and it may seem odd, therefore, that he did not prefer 'mental tone', mental 'disposition', or even the somewhat archaic 'humour'. Certainly 'emotion' is convenient in a literary sense, though Joachim notes that 'it sounds strange to talk of "active" and "passive" emotions, or of "emotions of desire".'[1] 'Disposition', indeed, has the additional advantage of emphasizing what is always essential to Spinoza's thought, the *agency* that is involved in ideas (for only agents can have dispositions), whereas 'emotion' (in spite of its etymology) is now too easily confused with mere passive 'feeling'. Not that 'disposition' is wholly unobjectionable, for it must be allowed that it is happier as applied to those *affectus* which bear relation to beings other than the mind to which the *affectus* belongs, e.g. desire, love, hate, etc., than to the simple *affectus* of joy and sadness which are ideas of transitional 'states' of the body itself. Nevertheless, these too are no mere 'feeling-contents', but in their way mental actions or endeavours.

Spinoza's own initial definition of '*affectus*' refers it primarily to the body: 'By *affectus* I understand the *affectiones* of the body by which the body's own power of acting is increased, diminished, aided or hindered, together with the ideas of these *affectiones*.'[2] But his main discussions are almost entirely in terms of the mental *affectus*, i.e. the ideas of the bodily *affectus*. Further, objection must be raised to the suggestion of the definition that the *affectus* are identical with *affectiones*, for when he comes to consider the primary *affectus* from which all others spring we find that so far

[1] *A Study of the Ethics of Spinoza*, p. 186. [2] *Eth. III, Def. iii.*

from these being *affectiones*, they are *transitions* from one 'state' to another more or less perfect, and the endeavour by which this transition is effected. Thus it would be truer to say that for Spinoza an *affectus* is, not the *affectio* by which greater or less perfection is conditioned, but the attaining of greater or less perfection involved in the change of *affectio*, or involving it. Though the *affectiones* which are the *termini* of the improvement or deterioration are, as *termini*, involved in the *affectus*, the *affectus* itself is the passage, or the endeavour by which it is conditioned, and the idea of it is the idea of the transition or endeavour.

Now, since all transitions and endeavours are durational, the ideas of the *affectus* are one and all inadequate: ideas of *Imaginatio*. The inadequacy of ideas of the body's *affectiones* lies in their confusion of the natures of the body and external things, but that of ideas of the body's *affectus* lies rather in their transitional nature: they are *summary* rather than *integral*. Though Spinoza's initial definition may serve well enough as a broad description, therefore, it needs some emendations in the light of what follows. The mental *affectus* are confused summary ideas of appraisement of the efficiency of the endeavouring body. I say 'appraisement' because they are concerned with the improvement or deterioration of the body's power or perfection—either its endeavour to *preserve* itself (which, in view of the powers which it has to face, involves an indefinite endeavour to *improve* itself) or its awareness of success or failure in that endeavour. Hence the *affectus* involve the conceptions of *natural* good and evil:[1] 'Knowledge of good and evil is nothing but the *affectus* of joy or sadness in so far as we are conscious of it.'[2]

Spinoza distinguishes three primary *affectus* which are original and simple from an indefinite remainder which spring from them by reason of the conditions under which the primary *affectus* are enjoyed or suffered or exerted. I shall call these 'derivative *affectus*' or 'mental dispositions', and examine the two kinds *seriatim*.

I. THE PRIMARY *AFFECTUS*

All the mental *affectus* or dispositions may be conceived as derived from, and involving, one or more of three primary *affectus*:

---

[1] To be distinguished from *moral* good and evil, the nature of which has yet to be considered: see below, Ch. IX.   [2] *Eth. IV, viii.*

H

desire, joy, and sadness. Desire is consciousness of endeavour
to preserve, and thus adequately to improve, one's own being.
This endeavour is the actual essence of the durational agent both
as mind and as body. Joy is the confused summary consciousness
of the transition of the mind and the body from a less to a greater
power or perfection; sadness the confused summary consciousness of their transition from a greater to a less power or perfection. In desire we have summary confused consciousness of the
agency of the self under the privation of self-reference as its
unfailingly perseverant *conatus* or actual durational essence; in
joy and sadness consciousness of the success or failure of that
conatus. Desire bears relation to the *affectiones* or confused ideas
involving the natures of self and other, and it thus includes all
the endeavours, impulses, appetites, and volitions of a man, which
vary according to his changing constitution, and thus 'not in-
frequently are so opposed to one another that a man is drawn
hither and thither and knows not which way to turn himself'.[1] As
to joy and sadness, these, as we have seen, are transitions, not
perfections or imperfections: 'I say "transition"; for joy is not
perfection itself. For if a man were born with the perfection to
which he passes he would possess it without the *affectus* of joy.
Which appears even more clearly from the *affectus* of sadness: for
that sadness consists in the transition to a less perfection, but not
in the less perfection itself, no one can deny, inasmuch as so far
as a man participates in any perfection, to that extent he cannot
be sad.'[2]

II. DERIVATIVE *AFFECTUS* OR MENTAL DISPOSITIONS

No complete account can be given of the *affectus* which spring
from the three primary sources under the indefinitely various
conditions of their durational actualization. For not only are they
countless,[3] but like the primary *affectus* they vary in character
from individual to individual of the same species, and from
species to species, even when they pass under the same name,[4]
nay, even from occasion to occasion in the same individual.[5]
Spinoza offers analyses of about half a hundred distinct types of

[1] *Eth. III, Affect. Def. i, Explic.*   [2] *Eth. III, Affect. Def. iii, Explic.*
[3] *Eth. III, lvi.*   [4] *Eth. III, lvii.*   [5] *Eth. III, lv.*

mental disposition experienced by man with respect to an other
in so far as this is inadequately conceived through his own
affectiones which confuse the natures of self and other. Such dispositions he calls 'passions' since they are 'related to man in so
far as he is passive', i.e. is imagined to be passive with respect to
the agreement or opposition of an other. Such dispositions are,
of course, imaginational, for the supposed other is indeed a
summary confusion of self and other.

Though Spinoza's analyses are full of interest, we need not
occupy time in setting them forth at length; but the general
principles of their derivativity are worth some exemplification
and consideration as a preparation for the proper understanding
of his doctrine of the mind's liberation from them.

1. *The Passions*

In the passions the transition to an imagined greater or less perfection takes its rise, not from the intrinsic endeavour of the
self, but from that of the imagined other. The most prominent
and fundamental examples are the passions of love and hatred:
love, he says, 'is only joy attending the idea of an external cause',
and hatred 'only sadness attending the idea of an external cause'.[1]
Both love and hatred entail desire—the one to preserve and
retain the cause, the other to destroy and remove it.[2] The supposed 'external cause' is, of course, imaginational, and even as
such only accidental through association:[3] a man may hate music,
e.g. because in his experience it has been associated with serious
illness. Again, a man may love or hate what only superficially
resembles something that joy or sadness has attended:[4] he may
even both love and hate the same thing if, in itself, its idea is
attended by joy, yet, as resembling something else, it is attended
by sadness. He will thus suffer a kind of 'affective doubt' or
vacillation of mind—a state common enough when we consider
the mind at large, because, as the 'idea of the body' which is composed of many members, it may pass to a greater perfection in
one member, and to a less perfection in another, by reason of the
same imagined external cause.[5] Such vacillation is, indeed,
characteristic of the mind as affected by passion, for it has many

[1] *Eth. III, xiii, Sch.*　　[2] *Eth. III, xxviii.*　　[3] *Eth. III, xiv; xv.*
[4] *Eth. III, xvi.*　　　　　　　　　　　　　　　　　　[5] *Eth. III, xvii, Sch.*

causes other than these: e.g. sadness attends the destruction or
deterioration of an object of love, and joy that of anything hated;
our love or hatred of a thing is qualified by the hatred or love,
respectively, of the same thing by one whom we love; and so on
—but let what has now been said about love, hatred, and vacillation suffice for our present purposes, not forgetting that all such
dispositions are attended by desire, which 'is greater as the
affectus is greater'.[1] And it is this desire which is the root of the
imaginational imputation of natural 'goodness' and 'badness' to
the imagined 'external causes'—for joy as such is desired, and sadness shunned, so that 'whatsoever conduces to joy is said to be
good, what conduces to sadness evil'; 'each according to his
affectus judges a thing to be good or evil'.[2] This judgement, as
thus determined, however, is essentially imaginational, and the
goodness or badness imputed is thus neither 'moral' nor true,
though it may well be 'evident'.

2. The 'Exertions'

So far we have considered the mental dispositions imaginationally attending our ideas of 'external causes'; but the cause of the
transition to a greater perfection must, primarily at least, be a
cause, i.e. a potency-in-act, intrinsic to the being itself (though
this, of course, being matched by the potency of its complement
in eternal Nature so far as it is constituted by community therewith, under self-reference is confusedly qualified by alien potency). And the actualization of this intrinsic potency in the life
of the durational being cannot but involve a transition to a greater
perfection which is apprehended as joy, and never as sadness,
attending the idea of the self. And in so far as this transition is
towards closer community with beings external to the self, a man is
apt, even as a durational agent, to imagine that he affects others
with joy accompanied by the idea of himself as cause. This is the
'active *affectus*' (as Spinoza calls it) of self-esteem, which as it is
perfected is one with 'tranquillity of mind').[3] On the other hand,
in so far as a man contemplates any privation of his potency-in-

[1] *Eth. III, xxxvii.*
[2] *Eth. III, xxxix, Sch.* See below, Chapter IX, sect. i.
[3] '*Acquiescentia in se ipso.*' 'Self-esteem' must be distinguished from self-
conceit.

act he is sad, and his sadness attending the idea of himself is humility,[1] which is a passion.

I have preferred to style the *affectus* which attend adequate ideas of self and complement 'exertions' rather than 'actions' because all the *affectus* are *durational* transitions and efforts rather than essential actions which are eternal. And in this no violence is done to Spinoza's intention, since the express purpose of the doctrine of 'active *affectus*' is to explicate the processes of moral liberation rather than to describe the nature of eternal life. Unlike the passions in which joy, sadness, and desire attend ideas that are inadequate, and are summary ideas of appraisement of the efficiency and power of the body as apprehended inadequately, or through its *affectiones*, which confuse its nature with that of other bodies, and their natures with its, the 'exertions' are dispositions in which joy and desire, but not sadness,[2] attend ideas that are adequate, or in so far as they are adequate, i.e. self-certifying, or *self-appraising*[3] as authentic. As *affectus*, they are still summary, and not integral, ideas of appraisement of the efficiency and the power of the body in so far as it is adequately apprehended, i.e. in constitutive community with members of its complement in Nature. I say 'in so far', because by the completion of this adequation of its ideas the mind would be wholly freed from *affectus*, and hence from mere 'exertion', and would enjoy the eternal 'blessedness' of the *creatum*.

These 'exertions' of the mind are epitomized by Spinoza as forms of 'steadfastness'[4] which by reason of the twin reference to self and complement inherent in the microcosmic constitution of the macrocosm, takes the form with respect to the self of 'strength of mind',[5] and with respect to others of 'magnanimity',[6] i.e. joyful desire, from the dictates of reason alone, both to preserve one's own being by thus increasing its perfection, and to give aid to others and to join them to oneself in friendship.

Thus, if it is asked (as it often has been asked) why a man whose actual durational essence is the endeavour to preserve his own being, should rationally desire the good and the friendship of others, the broad reply must be that man is a 'part' of Nature, and his power of acting is thus increased by association with its

---

[1] *Eth. III, lv, et Sch.* 'Humility' means pusillanimity rather than modesty.
[2] *Eth. III, lix.*   [3] See above, pp. 67–8.   [4] *Fortitudo* (*Eth.III, lix, Sch.*).
[5] *Animositas* (*loc. cit.*).   [6] *Generositas* (*loc. cit.*).

other 'parts' which agree with him in nature,[1] so that 'nothing can better agree with the nature of any being than others of the same species, . . . nothing is more useful to man for the preservation of his being, and the enjoyment of a rational life, than a man who is guided by reason';[2] and as to the vast majority of men, who are not so guided, their 'minds are not conquered by arms, but by love and magnanimity'.[3] 'Above all things it is profitable to man . . . to do that which serves to strengthen men's friendships.'[4]

But now the objection will be pressed that this reply makes of friendship nothing but disguised selfishness by which the other is subordinated to, not co-ordinated with, the self. And to this objection the reply must be that in so far as man is subject to unemended *Imaginatio* and ruled by his passions this is, indeed, a fair approximation to the truth; but in so far as he attains to true knowledge, or adequate ideas, the supposition of a gulf set between self and other becomes illegitimate. Thus as a man makes his way towards true liberation by way of 'exertions' he finds that only *genuine* friendship, co-ordinate with self-esteem, and not subordinate to self-love, is truly profitable to him, as not being self-defeating. And 'though men for the most part regulate all things by their inclination, yet many more advantages follow from their common fellowship; so that it is more satisfactory to bear with equanimity their injuries, and to apply our minds to those things which subserve concord and the production of friendship'.[5] But concord, with good faith (and not that which is founded on fear) is begotten by justice, integrity, and honour.[6]

This magnanimous pursuit of the good and friendship of others is but an approximation to the eternal constitutive community of all finite individual agents in the infinite Agent, or *causa sui*. For in such community of finites, the finite self has to do, not with a multiplicity of competing 'others', but with its complement in so far as it is *alter ego*, by community with which, not as 'thing' with 'thing', but as *agent* with *agent*, it is constituted. For though finite 'thinghood' implies separation, finite *agency* implies community.

---

[1] *Eth. IV, Appendix vii.*   [2] *Loc. cit., Appendix ix.*   [3] *Loc. cit., Appendix xi.*
[4] *Loc. cit., Appendix xii.*   [5] *Loc. cit., Appendix xiv.*   [6] *Loc. cit., Appendix xv, xvi.*

III. TOWARDS TRANQUILLITY OF MIND[1]

The privation and the vacillation which characterize human life in so far as it is under the guidance of the passions are analogous with the error and doubt to which *Imaginatio* is subject. Similarly we may justly assimilate the wise pursuit of imaginational things to the 'evidence' of those ideas of *Imaginatio* which, though not adequate, are yet not false but, as we say, 'factual'; and again, the experimental attitude which the lack of certain knowledge of the natures of such things renders profitable, with 'supposal'. Thus though 'the knowledge and love of God' is man's essential good,[2] yet 'to make use of things, and to delight in them as much as possible (not, however, *ad nauseam*, for this is not to be delighted) is proper to the wise man. I say it is proper to the wise man to refresh and renew himself with moderate and agreeable food and drink, and with perfumes, with the charm of verdant plants, with adornment and music and sports, theatres and other things of this kind, so as each man can without any harm to another. For the human body is composed of many parts of diverse nature, which continually need new and varied nourishment so that the whole body may be equally fit for all the things which can follow from its nature, and consequently that the mind also may be equally fit for understanding many things at once. This mode of living best agrees both with our principles and with common practice, so that if there are others, this plan of living is the best, and in every way to be commended.'[3]

Nevertheless it has its defects and its perils so far as men are subject to their passions. For even those passions which involve only joy and desire, excluding sadness, often produce vacillation of mind, unbalance, and satiety; and to these where sadness also is involved must be added impotence, subjection to fortune, and pulverulence of mind. Thus disquiet of mind is characteristic of the man whose desires are related to the passions, save in so far as by impotence he ceases to be a man.

Now, man in the 'common order of nature' cannot wholly eliminate his passions,[4] yet he is the more perfect as they are brought under control, for then he is less subject to fortune, more balanced in mind, more potent, less divided against

[1] *'Acquiescentia in se ipso.'*   [2] *Eth. IV, xxviii.*   [3] *Eth. IV, xlv, Sch.*
[4] *Eth. IV, iv, Cor.*

himself—in short, at once more efficient and more potently
tranquil in mind. We are not here considering how such a change
is possible,[1] and how expedited, but simply with Spinoza's
appraisement of the lives of passion and of 'exertion'. Man as
eternal *creatum*, i.e. in his finite perfection 'as referred to God', is
constituted by community with his congruent complement in
Nature—for this is implied by the nature of 'being' as *agent* and
not as 'thing'. Perfect mental agency is 'intellectual love', and
human perfection thus involves not merely tranquil intrinsic
efficiency but also, implied in this, an identification of self with
'other' as *alter ego*. Not that they are thus *merged* into a single
'thinghood', but *distinct* by reason of the requirements of *agency*
that is finite, so that *the more they are at one, the more they are
distinct*. So also in durational life, the more a man is guided by
'exertion', and enjoys self-esteem, the more he must contemplate
the other as estimable. Hence, as we saw, the epitomizing of the
'exertions' under the two heads of 'strength of mind' and 'magnanimity'. In so far as man's desires spring from these sources he
is delivered from vacillation, instability, impotence, satiety, subjection to fortune, pulverulence, and all such disquietudes of
mind, and attains that self-esteem which in its perfection is true
tranquillity of mind: '*acquiescentia in se ipso*'. This is no mere
state of impassibility, inertia, stupor, or self-satisfied obtundity,
but at once pure action, complete understanding, and perfect
adaptation to the self's congruent complement in Nature. 'He
who possesses a body adapted to many things has a mind the
greater part of which is eternal.'[2] 'He who, like an infant or a
boy, has a body adapted to very few things, and almost entirely
dependent on external causes, has a mind which, considered in
itself alone, is almost entirely unconscious of itself, and God, and
things. Contrariwise, he who has a body adapted to many things
has a mind which, considered in itself alone, is greatly conscious
of itself, and God, and things.'[3] But that perfect tranquillity of
mind that Spinoza calls 'blessedness' is not to be enjoyed *sub
specie durationis*, but at best approximated to in the durational
form of 'a joy continuous and supreme for eternity';[4] for man

---

[1] Nor was Spinoza in *Eth. III, xliii*, the proposition in which, according to de
Burgh (following Guzzo, *Il pensiero di B. Spinoza*, pp. 290–1) he begged the
whole question of morals.
[2] *Eth. V, xxxix*.   [3] *Eth. V, xxxix, Sch.*   [4] *Tract. de Intell. Emend.*, § 1.

is but a 'part' of Nature, the other 'parts' of which are vastly more potent, and this partiality as it is expressed in the 'common order of nature' in his self-referent perspective determines the limits of his *conatus* in comparison with external causes,[1] and the degree in which he can eradicate his passions within the limits of his comparative potency.[2] For by his self-reference the inequality of the potencies of self and other is not moderated but exacerbated, and the self's efforts after emendation to 'reference to God' cannot but be obstructed by the like self-reference of the other (for he suffers from the multilateral self-reference of the multiplex complement—a situation that tends to be concealed by Spinoza's own 'rational' approach). Thus, by no 'exertion' of his own can he attain full liberation: he must 'endure with equanimity the injuries inflicted' by others while applying his mind 'to those things which subserve concord, and the establishment of friendship'; but he must not expect to be able to do so without being affected by indignation, fear, pity, and the like, or without cultivating hope, emulation, benevolence, courtesy, and the like. One class of passion alone must be excluded if he is rightly to apply his mind, viz. hatred and all those involving it: derision, scorn, envy, vengeance, cruelty, etc.; for 'hatred can never be good',[3] nor is anything truly hateful.[4] Let a man 'do well and rejoice'[5] and he will thus gain, as far as it is possible, tranquillity of mind, with his conscience 'like a sea at rest'. But the question remains: how is this liberation, not merely possible, but effectively and rationally pursued under the conditions of durational life?

[1] *Eth. IV, iii.*   [2] *Eth. IV, iv, Cor.*   [3] *Eth. IV, xlv.*
[4] *Eth. IV, l, Sch.*   [5] *Loc. cit.*

PART III

THE DOCTRINE OF LIBERATION

CHAPTER IX

THE MORAL PREDICAMENT

No error in the common interpretation of Spinoza's thought is more fundamental than that which conceives his philosophy as a mechanistic determinism camouflaged by an incoherently super-imposed moralism. His doctrine, as we have seen, is essentially activistic, and is deterministic only because, and in the sense that, to 'act' *is* to determine. Thus for him mechanism is but the lower ideal limit of existence: excluding action, it determines only non-existence. It is because for Spinoza reality is agency, and durational being conation, which is a privation of agency, that morality is of essential moment in 'this present life'.

And indeed, no great mental acuity is demanded for the recognition of the truth that if all events are taken (*per impossibile*) as transeuntly determined *a tergo*, the behaviour of an individual (i.e. the events falling within the contours of his being) cannot be free in any sense other than the purely nominal one that many of the 'causes' also fall within those contours. For in the end the 'causes' of even these lie wholly beyond the nature of the individual. Nor can such transeuntly determined behaviour be *ethically* evaluated. True, we might say that the individual's behaviour is 'profitable' or 'unprofitable' to him, i.e. that it conduces to, or detracts from, his power to survive in a given environment; but this judgement is relative and economic, not ethical save on the assumption that the given environment sets an ethical standard—an assumption discredited, or at least rebutted, by the judgement that the behaviour of the individual is moral or immoral in so far as it so modifies the given environment as to make it more or less fitted for the survival of the individual: i.e. that the individual sets the ethical standard. The mutual fitness or unfitness of individual and environment is essentially relative, whereas ethical evaluation requires a standard that is in some sense absolute, a norm to which individual, environment, and their relations ought to, but do or do not, approximate. I say 'ought', for mere approximation or otherwise without this is nothing—a lion is not ill-formed because his neck is shorter than that of a giraffe, though he would be if it were as long. The standard must be appropriate.

Further, though we may conceive it to be possible that mechanistic determination might assemble more or less permanent conformations of events such as a solar system, a molecule, or even, perhaps, a society, capable of more or less independent survival in a changing environment, yet on the mechanistic assumption such assemblages would not be effective individuals at all, but mere contours of complex transeuncy. Their 'self-determination' would be merely nominal, i.e. only the transeunt 'effect' under environmental conditions, of what predated them.

Mechanistic determinism thus affords no ground for ethical judgement—for even ethical relativism is founded on the assumption of relative individual efficiency; and this, on the mechanistic hypothesis, is chimerical. 'Individuals' that are no more than nominal contours of transeuncies, whose behaviour is the complex resultant of transeunt 'causes' nominally included within their contours, cannot be ethically valued. Indeed, we can go further and claim that the very notion of extrinsic determination, pure and simple, is unintelligible and void; that mechanistic determinism presupposes what it denies, viz. that intrinsically effective individuals operate transeuntly. 'Causality' that is purely transeunt, as Hume saw clearly enough, is chimerical. Genuine causality is not transeunt coercion, but immanent expression, or the actualization of potency; and the transeuncy of durational causality is a privation, under self-reference, of the real causality, or agency, of the 'proximate cause' of both transeunt 'cause' and 'effect'.

Moral evaluation, then, presupposes effective individuality. But no less it also presupposes a certain privation of effectiveness and individuality, conjoined with the availability of a capacity to transcend these limitations. 'Good' and 'bad', 'better' and 'worse', signify approach to, or recession from, a norm of efficiency and individuality, an *exemplar* of proper perfection. Indeed, this is true even of what I have called 'economic' evaluation—the judgement of utility or inutility—though here the *exemplar* is the extant individual seeking profit, under the imagination of self with desire fulfilled. And the judgement falls short of ethical import by reason of its uncritical imaginational *exemplar*: for the truly 'moral' judgement requires a *moral exemplar* embodying a *true* good, or a *truly* better, by approximation to which the individual is to be valued.

In *Ethices III* Spinoza, we saw, identified 'good in general' with the object of desire: 'We neither strive for, wish, seek, nor desire anything because we think it to be good, but on the contrary, we judge a thing to be good because we strive for, wish, seek, or desire it.'[1] This statement has often suggested to the unwary that for Spinoza 'good' and 'bad' are merely 'economic' conceptions relative to extant, durational, individual essence. Nor need we go so far as to assert that this suggestion is *wholly* false (for the preservation of the durational self is *prima facie* the *sine qua non* of the good durational life, and actual desire its extant essence); but it is plainly false when it is conceived as the sufficient ground of moral evaluation, since it affords no foundation for the distinction of *true* and *apparent* good and evil—a distinction in the light of which even durational self-preservation may be subject to revaluation—the economic being subordinated to the moral.

This distinction is clearly enunciated in the *Preface* to *Ethices IV* where the argument passes from 'psychology' to ethics. 'As to good and evil', he says, 'these terms indicate nothing positive in things considered in themselves, nor are they anything else than modes of thought, or notions, which we form from the comparison of one thing with another. For one and the same thing may at the same time be both good and evil, or indifferent. . . . But although this is so, we must retain these words. For since we desire to form for ourselves an idea of man upon which we may look as an *exemplar* of human nature, it will be of service to us to retain these terms' (in the following senses): 'By *good* I understand in what follows everything which we are certain is a means by which we may approach nearer and nearer to the *exemplar* of human nature which we set before us. By *evil*, on the contrary, I understand everything which we are certain hinders us from reaching that *exemplar*.' And what is most important in view of his destructive criticism, in the *Appendix* to *Ethices I*, of the ideas of 'good', 'evil', 'order', 'confusion', 'beauty', 'deformity', etc., as commonly applied to things in nature, because these appraisements arise from the illegitimate measurement of the nature and power of things against criteria extrinsic to the

[1] *Eth. III, ix, Sch.*

natures of the things appraised, he is careful to add that this
moral *exemplar* is not something other than the individual that is
compared with it—for then approach to it, or recession from it,
would mean change to an alien nature, and not the betterment or
the worsening of existing nature—but is his true, complete, or
perfect nature, undefected and unobstructed, i.e. since all obstruction stems from unilateral self-reference, the *exemplar* is the
individual 'as referred to God'.

Many, if not all, of the difficulties that have beset students of
the ethical doctrine of Spinoza have arisen from failure to grasp
the relation, on his principles, between durational beings and the
eternal *creata* of which they are self-referent, and therefore privative, expressions. For creation is eternal, not temporally repeti-
tive or continuous. The durational conator is thus rooted in the
eternal real, partially alienated therefrom, and struggling under
its diminished *nisus* for realization. Its 'field' of endeavour, its
partially co-operative and partially obstructive other, is its alienated complement, the realization of which concurs with the
realization of self. 'This present life,' therefore, is at once partially self-subjected to transeuncy, and involves an endeavour,
well or ill-directed, towards release from transeuncy. It is
neither a tissue of impotencies wholly subjected to transeuncy *a
tergo*, i.e. a mechanism, nor is it a realm of 'free necessity *ab
intra*', neither indeterminacy nor free necessity, but electively
bifurcated and moral.

We have, therefore, not to assimilate a contour of impotencies
oddly miscalled an 'empirical self', with a self-governing real self
by means of a posited supervenient 'morality' having no essential
relation with either, but, in the light of its etiology, to understand the privative nature of the durationally endeavouring self
seeking self-preservation within a more or less alien field by
means well or ill directed, i.e. by inclinations attending passions
or by efforts attending 'exertions', according to its original status
in Nature (moderating the privation that it suffers under self-
reference) and the self-emendation that it has achieved. For if
this is accomplished there will remain no opposition between the
'positive' assertions of *Ethices III et IV*, and the 'moral' assertions of the first part of *Ethices V*.

Let us now consider in somewhat greater detail the manner in
which these assertions are to be understood as consistent.

I. DESIRE AND GOOD

Much has been made in recent times of the dangers of allowing linguistic forms of expression unduly to influence philosophical beliefs—though these perils have always been recognized by critical philosophers. It does not follow that because 'this is yellow' and 'this is good' are identical in grammatical form, 'yellow' and 'good' are attributes of things in the same sense and manner.[1] This particular error is the more difficult to recognize because, though no one can fail to notice that the same thing can be both good and bad (and indifferent) *for* different people, and *for* the same man at different times, it is equally true that the same thing can appear as yellow, as brown, as grey, etc., *to* different people, and *to* the same man at different times. Nevertheless, the change of the preposition imports recognition of the essential distinction of 'fact' and 'value'. When we say that a thing is yellow we attribute yellowness to it independently of any advantage or disadvantage that may accrue (though not, perhaps, independently of the nature of the percipient), whereas when we say that it is good we attribute goodness to it only in relation to that *for* which it is good. We may say '*to* me this is yellow though *to* you it is grey', but we say '*for* me this is good though *for* you it is bad'. To take 'good' as a 'factual attribute' is to overlook its relativity as imputed—to take what is good for one or another, as good in itself without reference to the advantage which its possession is taken to yield to one or another. Though it may well be argued that 'yellow' means only 'yellow *to*', 'good' means not merely 'good to', but 'good *for*'.

It follows, therefore, that we do not desire a thing because we recognize independent goodness in it, but we judge it to be good because we desire it—desire being essentially related to advantage For 'desire' here means any kind of conscious effort, and is the 'actual essence' of the durational mind, so that it cannot be consciously self-destructive. We do not 'desire' that which we take to be harmful, but at best 'accept it with aversion' for the sake of some greater or more essential advantage. And here it must carefully be noted that this is not an ethical, but a psychological,

[1] It is odd that G. E. Moore, an influential leader of the recent linguistic movement in philosophy, appears himself to fall into this error (cf. *Principia Ethica*, § 7).

I

principle, and thus affords no inescapable basis for ethical egoism, save on the assumption of a false theory of the relation of self and other. Desire for a thing involves, we may say, an implicit judgement, true or false, that it is profitable; and the explicit judgement that it is good does no more than explicate the nature of the desire.

But now it will, perhaps, be urged that this doctrine implies that all 'good' is 'good as means', yet that unless something is 'good absolutely' nothing *can* be 'good as means'. An infinite regress of means to no end is vicious, and the goodness of that which is good only for what is indifferent is not merely relative but illusory. *I* may call a thing 'good', taking it to be advantageous to me, because my being and its advantage is to me *relatively absolute*; but to establish conviction that the goodness of the thing is not *absolutely relative*, it must be shown that my being and its advantage is good in itself, or at least good as means to what is good in itself.

That there is an important truth in this objection need not be denied, and is not denied by Spinoza—though the truth lies *perdue*. For though a man is good *in* himself in so far as he is good *for* himself (i.e. acts so as to preserve and improve himself), yet this goodness is only *relatively* absolute, for durational betterment is not eternal perfection. The goodness of the desiring self is its capacity for improvement; and *sub specie durationis* this subservience to betterment cannot be transcended; so that for the durational conator good is essentially relative—and not excluding his own goodness on which that of the objects of his desire is founded. For a being incapable of betterment would be no durational conator but a perfect eternal agent, even though finite. Yet the distinction of good and bad is not *absolutely* relative, i.e. illusory; on the contrary, the durational effort after improvement emanates from an eternal perfection never durationally attainable, but always effective as more or less privative *nisus*. And to this perfection all durational endeavour is more or less defectively asymptotic. Thus all *conatus*, as the pursuit of what is taken to be profitable, is *implicitly* 'moral'; it becomes specifically and *explicitly* moral in the degree in which it is truly enlightened and the distinction between 'apparent' and 'true' good adequately developed; and its moral imperative lies in the actual *nisus* to eternal perfection.

II. APPARENT AND TRUE GOOD

We have seen that when Spinoza turns to explicitly ethical inquiry, he distinguishes between 'good in general' and 'certain
good', between 'bad in general' and 'certain bad'. Good and bad
in general are 'every kind of joy, and what conduces to it', and
'every kind of sadness', respectively.[1] True good, however, is
'that which we *certainly know* to be profitable to us', and the truly
bad 'that which we *certainly know* to hinder us from possessing
anything that is good'.[2] That is to say, morality involves an
exemplar through which we distinguish true from apparent good
and evil.

It may, perhaps, be thought that in introducing the notion of a
rational *exemplar* Spinoza is denying his own principle that a
thing must be judged by what it is, so that everything is as perfect as it is its nature to be. The durational conator is just that,
and comparison with a moral *exemplar* therefore illegitimate. As
against this objection, however, it must be noted that for Spinoza
the durational conator is never 'just that', not even when he is
conceived as morally unawakened. As a self-referent privation of
an eternal *creatum* his 'actual essence' involves a *nisus* to improvement, so that the moral *exemplar* is not something superadded,
but is already inchoate in his durational character and situation.
Conatus is no principle of inertia, but of agency by which it is
perseverant and adaptable to an environment partly obstructive
and partly co-operant. It thus, as such, implicitly sets for itself
an *exemplar* of some sort, viz. itself adjusted to its changing environment so as to maintain its being, and to maximize its power
in relation to its field. Morality, therefore, is the rational explica-
tion of this essential effort, and its *exemplar* the rational emendation and realization of what is durationally, not absent, but
inchoate. It is no supervenient order extraneously imposed on a
mechanistic temporal extancy, but its negation—it is the rational
development and correction of the very essence of durational
conatus. For this is the pursuit of what *seems evidently* good; but
morality is the pursuit of what is *certainly* good, and which, as
probing through the seeming, involves a *choice*, though not a
'*free decision*'. Full recognition of the indifference or the certain badness of what seems to be good would, of course, eliminate

[1] *Eth. III, xxxix, Sch.*   [2] *Eth. IV, Deff. i et ii.*

choice, which occurs only under the conditions of durational discovery, though there it is evident enough.

That Spinoza's introduction of the moral *exemplar* seems divorced from the principles expounded in *Ethices III* arises from his 'rational' procedure—for the *Ethics* is, of course, in the main, an expression of the 'second kind of knowledge' or *Ratio*. Thus, what he puts forward is the exemplar of 'man' or of 'human nature', not of this or that man. And this is applicable to this or that man only *qua* man. A man's concrete *exemplar* is himself as fully emended, as 'referred to God'. Morality is thus the emendation of his inchoate imaginational *exemplar*, the verification of good, the activation of *conatus*, the adequation of the causality of the self, its enfranchizement.

III. THE NATURE AND STATUS OF EVIL

Since according to Spinoza the effort of all durational things is always for that which is profitable, and the profitable is what we call 'good', it has often been supposed that for him evil can *be* nothing but defective good. It is, of course, true that he denies that desire, i.e. conscious effort, can be for what is certainly known, or taken without doubt, to be unprofitable, that is (as the phrase goes) that all pursuit is *sub ratione boni* (though Spinoza would rather say that all good is *sub ratione cupiditatis*). In the same way it has been thought that for him error can *be* no more than defective truth, i.e. partial ignorance, and this is the interpretation often put on his statement that 'Falsity consists in the *privation* of knowledge'.[1] In the correspondence with van Blyenbergh[2] he makes similar statements about sin or moral evil, but there the issue is confused because he is considering what sin in man is in relation to God, rather than what it is in relation to the sinning man. This is not the place for attempting any full *éclaircissement* of his use of the term 'privation', but it must certainly be allowed that it is somewhat confusing, if not ambiguous. In *Epistola xxi*, e.g., he says that privation is 'only a simple and mere lack, which in itself is nothing'; but later, in the same letter, he says that it is 'nothing but the denying of a thing something which we judge to pertain to its nature', so that it differs from 'negation' only in so far as this is 'denying of a thing

---

[1] *Eth. II, xxxv.* [2] *Epp. xviii–xxiv, xxvii.*

something because it does not belong to its nature'. This conflict is, of course, resolved if, without qualification, it is denied that anything can pertain to a thing's nature which is not fully actual.

It is not at all clear whether these seeming ambiguities are examples of Spinoza's celebrated laconicism, or whether they indicate a passing stage in the *approfondissement* of his thought. That they are not absent from the *Ethics*[1] lends colour to the former suggestion; and in that case we have reason to regret (though not, perhaps, to complain) that he did not go out of his way to emphasize sufficiently the distinct standpoints in relation to which his accounts, and uses, of the term 'privation' are to be justified and reconciled—especially in view of his unqualified strictures of vulgar ideas in the *Appendix* to *Ethices I*. In the correspondence with van Blyenbergh, the difficulties of his correspondent arise from his failure to keep strictly to the question of *God*'s relation to human sin and evil, assuming that the *sinner*'s relation to his sin must be the same: if it is defect to God it can be nothing but defect to man; if positive to man, then positive also to God. That Spinoza did not plainly convict van Blyenbergh of this fallacy suggests that his own mind was not fully clarified at that time. And yet, when he described error as distinct from ignorance and as a privation of knowledge,[2] his mind cannot have been other than clear about these distinctions.

Let us attempt, then, in our own way to clarify them. If, *per impossibile*, we consider man as *merely* durational, plainly we are not justified in attributing to him any power not durationally actual, so that from that standpoint privation and defect are indiscernible. Again, if we consider the relation of durational man to God from whom all his positive essence is derived, any defect in his nature, whether it marks his finite status in Nature,

[1] E.g., *Eth. III, Aff. Def. iii, Explic.*, which denies that sadness 'consists in the privation of a greater perfection' because 'privation is nothing' whereas sadness is something actual. But it is surely not illegitimate to describe the *passage* to a less perfect state as a 'privation' so long as 'privation' is not interpreted as necessarily involving the comparison of incomparable things (of a blind man, e.g., or a stone, with a man who sees). Certainly, for Spinoza sadness is not the mere *absence* of a greater perfection—this, indeed, is what he is emphasizing in this passage: it is a *transition* to a less perfect state, and, surely, a *privative* transition.

[2] *Eth. II, xxxv, Dem.* The common habit of infecting this proposition with the ambiguities discussed above, instead of attempting to clarify the ambiguities in the light of what it clearly asserts, will hardly commend itself to the candid student.

or results from the privative efforts put forth under self-reference, can be nothing positive from the divine standpoint, and implies no privation in God. But when we consider man as an eternal *creatum* partially self-deprived by self-reference we are justified in comparing his durational actuality with the eternal actuality thus clouded, diminished, and fragmented, and distinguishing the 'defect' which marks only his finiteness, and the 'privation' which constitutes his badness. And in so far as this is the standpoint of the man himself as moral agent, for him his evil deeds are not mere defects but privations of his finite perfection. I say 'in as far as', for he is *morally* bad only in so far as his chosen deeds fall short of his principles.

Thus, just as in error there is assertion or assent without certification or 'evidence', so in moral evil there is desire without justification; and this is the sinner's own affair, and cannot be imputed to God—not even though self-reference, the 'original sin', is an expression of finite selfhood: for it is a *defective* expression, one 'moment' only of creaturely status, which can find completion only through 'reference to God'. For God does not create man as sinning, but as capable of the self-privation that is sin. And this, for the man himself, is no mere defect (for vice is not the mere absence of virtue), though for God, as creator, it is no more. It is thus that sin and error are *parasitical* on virtue and truth, for there is no *conatus* that is not the efflux of eternal potency-in-act, and no idea that is not the efflux of understanding. Nero's matricide was sinful, not as mere matricide (which is common enough in nature without the attribution of sin), and not as a mere deed (for the power by which it was accomplished was, as we say, God-given), but because 'it showed that he was ungrateful, unmerciful, and disobedient',[1] i.e. he transgressed against principles that he knew to be proper to his nature as a man. He 'chose the worse, though knowing the better', though not by 'free decision'.

Spinoza's doctrine of freedom, however, is too important to be introduced at the end of this chapter; let it suffice, therefore, to say that the denial of free, i.e. indifferent, decision in no way implies a denial of moral choice between inclination and principle, nor that it is illusory, i.e. has no kind or degree of freedom, though plainly it is not pure freedom, i.e. unhindered action. For

[1] *Ep. xxiii.*

the doctrine of *conatus* is not mechanistic, and all agency, however privative, involves its own kind and degree of freedom. Moral choice is certainly neither indifferent nor unhindered, but it is not therefore extrinsically compelled—for thus it would not be 'choice'.[1]

In sum, then, in all endeavour as subject to moral appraisement there is a more or less distinct bifurcation of selfhood as the agent's bias towards self-reference is 'dubitated' through the operation of the *nisus* to self-emendation, always in some measure durationally available, and more or less expressive of eternal community under 'reference to God'. It is the resolution of this bifurcation that is called 'moral choice', which is not to be conceived as a 'free decision' by the agent between extrinsic options, but as the very mode of the durational agent's conative being— not what he then *does*, but what he then *is* as a moral agent under the conative 'dubitation' proper to his extant durational nature and status. In so far as this involves the rejection of one or other mode of resolution, his endeavour is morally good or bad: the rejection of emendation is resolution by way of vice or enfeeblement, and the evil thus determined, though actualizing the depleted potency of the self-referent agent—which is fontally positive and by nature good—as essentially a privation of a better (and in the end of a perfection) must yet be judged to be, not the proper fruition of an agent so constituted and derived, but *parasitical* on the potency which is its *sine qua non*. For though in part it expresses, it does not corroborate, the potency of the agent. On the other hand, the pursuit of emendation is resolution by way of virtue or strength, and the good thus determined both expresses and corroborates the potency from which it springs.

[1] These topics are further elaborated below, Chapter XII, section ii.

CHAPTER X

EMENDATION

All finite beings as fully created, i.e. 'as referred to God', are eternal, and stand in need of no emendation. It is the finite agent as it suffers the privation arising from unilateral self-reference that requires, and, well or ill, must seek such emendation as will moderate or make good this privation. This durational *nisus* to emendation stems from the eternal finite perfection of the agent as *creatum* which is inherent in his privative state in the measure of his grade of finite perfection (for the higher the grade the less the privation resulting from self-reference), and of his accomplished emendation as durational—that is, it is inherent as ineluctable self and as *affectus*.

It has already been noticed that Spinoza's procedure in *Ethices IV–V* is 'rational', and, indeed, the *Ethics* in the main falls under the 'Second Kind of Knowledge'. It is thus that the ethical doctrine seems somewhat ambiguous as the rational principles receive application to the situation of this or that individual under this or that set of circumstances. There is a danger, which, perhaps, Spinoza does not wholly escape, of attempting to apply the abstract principles to concrete situations without due adaptation to their requirements—an error which can only result in the need for a compromise of principle in practice that morality cannot tolerate. Even the celebrated proposition: 'Hatred can never be good',[1] even as explicitly limited to 'hatred towards men',[2] though it has exemplary force, is apt to prove somewhat unrealistic in actual practice,—a defect which can hardly be met by distinguishing the man from his deeds and motives.

This danger can only be satisfactorily avoided by distinguishing clearly between abstract or 'exemplary' morality and concrete, applied, or 'mutual' ethics conceived, not as involving concession or compromise, but as the concrete embodiment of principle. For the moral agent and his *exemplar* of *Ethices IV* are 'man' and 'man's *exemplar*', not 'this or that man' and his *exemplar*; and the

[1] *Eth. IV, xlv.* [2] *Eth. IV, xlv, Sch.*

exemplar for each man is not, any more than the man himself,
an *ens rationis* but an *ens reale*, viz. the man himself 'as referred to
God', i.e. as *creatum*. It follows that the self-reference from
which each man suffers is not solely, but only primarily, his own,
it is the multiplex self-reference of all related beings; so that in
the absence of *general* emendation, the efforts of this or that man,
however vigorous and successful, are unable to ensure for him
full liberation, or even that degree of freedom which would result
from a fully co-operant 'field'. The conditions of individual
mutuality cannot be ignored merely on the ground that individual perfection reciprocates with perfection of congruent complement—indeed, this is the prime reason why it cannot be
rationally ignored.

Now, although Spinoza does not clearly distinguish 'exemplary' and 'mutual' ethics, the distinction is implicit in what he
says about the various endeavours of the 'man who is guided by
reason': for though there are some things that such a man always,
or never, does, there are others that he will strive to do, or to
avoid, 'as much as possible'—though inevitably this has the
appearance of compromise.[1] Further, the true sting of the *Axiom*
and early propositions of *Ethices IV* which emphasize the relative
weakness of individual men in nature, by reason of which their
efforts are hindered and may come to naught, lies just in this: for
human finiteness can be no source of peril in eternal *Natura*, but
only in the 'common order of nature' by reason of self-reference
through which durational men are not only self-stultified but also
in consequence rendered liable to hindrance and destruction *sub
specie durationis* by others, which as thus alienated, are both
rendered dangerous, and also, *under their own self-reference*, more
effectively hostile to the self-stultified self.

For these reasons I shall distinguish the essential principle of
emendation as it concerns this or that man under his own unilateral self-reference, by which his complement is defected to
otherness more or less hostile, and without reference to similar
privation in the other, which is thus conceived as emendable
solely by the emendation of the self—from the modes of its durational actualization in a world which suffers *distributive*, and thus
multilateral, self-reference and privation under the multiplex
unilateral self-reference of its manifold parts. We shall thus

[1] Cf. *Eth. IV, lxx, Sch.*

distinguish abstract or 'exemplary ethics' from concrete or 'mutual ethics' which approximate in form and degree 'as much as possible' to 'exemplary' principle as these multiplex conditions of durational life permit—not by way of compromise or concession or expediency, but by way of appropriate expression, rational adaptation, or duty under the actual conditions of durational mutuality. For this actual way to liberty of mind is 'steep and difficult', and for the most part no emendation of this or that individual mind, no 'Damascus-vision', without regard to the general 'scotomy' of men, will serve the requirements of morality—save, perhaps, as inspiring example where the conditions are favourable, or the agent heroic: for otherwise, not inspiration, but discouragement, is likely to be the outcome.

I. ITS ESSENTIAL PRINCIPLE: 'EXEMPLARY ETHICS'

Only by understanding the etiology and status of the durational agent can its power of self-emendation be estimated. Its self-privation under self-reference bears inverse relation to its elevation of status in *Natura*: for self-reference is proper only to *Natura* in relation to which it involves no privation, being identical with 'reference to God'. Thus the further removed the finite agent is from infinite perfection, the more it stands in need of the correction of self-reference by 'reference to God'. It is with man, a finite agent of middle status that we are now concerned. For him self-reference involves a certain bifurcation, so that he is at once partly subject to 'passion' and partly capable of 'exertion'. His freedom is not 'free necessity', but the quasi-freedom that we call 'choice'. This choice is not 'free', i.e. undetermined, 'decision'—not subjection to, or the breaking of, a deterministic chain of mechanistic 'causes' *a tergo*, but the expression of finite being bifurcated by self-privation. He does not *'make* a choice'; his extant being is expressed *as* a choice which is self-emending or self-impairing. The self-emending choice is a closer approximation to 'free necessity' than is a self-impairing choice; the latter a closer approximation to indeterminate contingency than the former. But every choice, as a mode of agency, has its degree of freedom; for freedom *is* agency: the actualization of potency. Thus, we have not to explain how a being embedded in mechanism can achieve a freedom thereby excluded, how the deterministic 'chain' of 'causes' can be broken; for the supposed 'chain' is but the 'ideal limit' of finite impotence nowhere extant. Spinoza would agree with Hume that in purely transeunt 'causes' there is no power.

Further, moral progress or retrogression under the microcosmic *nisus* inherent in the durational moral agent is not automatic or inevitable, though the *nisus* is always at work effectively or injuriously: effectively, as choice is of the truly better; injuriously, as it is of the worse, which, falsely judged as better, is a parasitically positive evil. Unemended *conatus* is the microcosmic *nisus* operating ignorantly, erroneously, or dubiously; and its emendation consists, not in its impairment, but in its enlightenment or concentration. It is thus that, though a desire attending 'passion' can only be overcome by one attending an 'exertion' (or, of course, by one attending a stronger 'passion')[1] the essential root of morality is the 'emendation of the intellect'. But though it is the 'essential root' it is not the durational expression of morality, which is the resolution of the conflict of 'passion' and 'exertion', for 'knowledge of good or evil is nothing but an *affectus* of joy or sadness in so far as we are conscious of it'.[2] Thus, *sub specie durationis*, 'passion' is not corrected by pure knowledge as such, but by 'exertion'; so that it becomes clear how far, and in what manner, the moral agent can 'know the better and yet choose the worse'. He can do so because his 'knowledge' of the better is not adequate or self-certifying, but imaginational—for there is no real choice between a certain and a dubious good, but only between a reputed good and the object of an urgent desire attending 'passion' or other *affectus*. Only inadequate knowledge can be morally ineffective. Moral choice involves 'knowledge of good and evil', i.e. the *affectus* of joy and sadness *more or less* certified, i.e. more or less verified by the 'emendation of the intellect'. Nero's matricide was sinful, that of a brute not, because, and in so far as, unlike the brutes, he had knowledge of good and evil, not, indeed, adequate, yet not wholly illusory, but inadequate, imaginational, though 'evident' enough: no mere hearsay maxim, but the doctrine of respected teachers which, free from 'passion', he would not have doubted or wished to oppose. In this fashion, 'knowing' the better, his extant nature was such as to choose the worse.

[1] *Eth. IV, vii.*   [2] *Eth. IV, viii.*

The opposition, therefore, of duty and inclination (to use the Kantian expressions) is not one of principle against force *a tergo*: it is the very form of the bifurcated pseudo-cognizant durational conator; and his choice is his actual durational essence, and not his undetermined decision. From this actuality he can only escape by the 'emendation of his intellect', or by the alternative way of the vulgar—by obedience to venerated authority: the 'prophets' or the *civitas* ('obedience' being distinguished from 'subjection', as involving 'exertion' and not mere 'passion'). But both the philosophic and the vulgar ways are 'steep and difficult', demanding perseverant moral choice, and not attainable by 'free decisions'. It is by right choosing that righteousness is corroborated, and by wrong choosing that parasitical vice gains strength; and both ways are always in some measure open.

Spinoza's *moral* doctrine is thus neither mechanistic nor intellectual. Pure mechanism is pure nonentity; but he is careful not to flout all experience by passing to the opposite extreme by asserting that pure knowledge as such can subdue the 'passions'. The durational power of knowledge lies in the 'exertions': but this does not mean that choice is determined by the superior strength of this or that *affectus* operating as a force *a tergo*; for thus there would be no 'choice' at all. Knowledge of the better, again, does not, according to Spinoza, only become effective by its chance association with some existing, and extraneous, force or impulse, as some critics have supposed, but by its intrinsic conative power *vis-à-vis* that of a contrary desire recognized as relatively worse. Choice is the expression of effective *conatus*, and neither a 'resultant' of forces nor an undetermined 'free' decision. And it is 'moral' in so far as naïve desire is subjected to axiological criticism more or less remotely based on the agent's eternal *exemplar*: the *Deus quatenus finitus est* that is the fontal essence of his durational actuality.

It remains, briefly and summarily to indicate the exemplary principles of the rational guidance of life for a man abstractedly conceived as living in a world partially alienated from him by reason of his own self-reference, and which is thus hostile to him in so far only as its true nature, and his own, are privatively apprehended, i.e. without consideration of the privation and hostility towards him that must be attributed to the intrinsic self-reference of the other. By this abstraction the principles of

'exemplary morality' are isolated. Such principles may be summarily expressed as the control of blind 'passion' by the development of rational 'exertion', for this is the imperfect imaginational
expression of the 'emendation of the intellect'—the essential distinction of 'passion' and 'exertion' being that the former is
intellectually myopic, but the latter intellectually visive; the one
attends inadequate, and the other adequate, ideas. More particularly, we may say that 'exemplary morality' requires that a man
should strive, by 'referring all things to God', after true understanding of himself and of things as divine *creata*;[1] after agreement with his other;[2] after the mutual adaptation of self and
other for the increase of mutual responsiveness;[3] after the integration of his own nature;[4] after increase of *affectus* of joy or
cheerfulness, and the suppression of melancholy,[5] but the moderation of ill-proportioned partial excitements of joy or sadness;[6]
and, above all, after the elimination of all hatred towards men[7]—
for to hate the other is to ascribe to him the privation which, *ex
hypothesi*, is determined solely by the self. And with hatred there
go envy, mockery, contempt, anger, indignation, revenge, etc.,
which all involve or arise from hatred, which seeks destruction
rather than understanding. Finally, 'exemplary morality' finds
no place for pity,[8] for dependence on hope,[9] for action from fear,[10]
or for deception.[11]

II. MODES OF ITS DURATIONAL ACTUALIZATION

But man's actual moral predicament is vastly more complex than
that which has thus been considered, for all durational men are
infected with self-referent privation, and the principles of
'exemplary morality', though never negated, are modalized to
meet this complex situation. Its dictates, Spinoza often says, must
be followed 'as much as possible'. We have reason, I think, to
cavil at this, his favourite, phrase, inasmuch as it inevitably suggests that actual conditions call for concessions and compromise.
But morality makes no concessions, and can tolerate no compromise. Unless, therefore, concrete 'mutual ethics' can be shown
to be the rational, uncompromising, expression of 'exemplary'

---

[1] *Eth. IV, xxvi; xxvii.*   [2] *Eth. IV, xxxii–xxxv.*   [3] *Eth. IV, xxxviii.*
[4] *Eth. IV, xxxix.*   [5] *Eth. IV, xlii.*   [6] *Eth. IV, xliii–xliv.*
[7] *Eth. IV, xlv et Cor. ii.*   [8] *Eth. IV, l.* See below, p. 127, note 1.
[9] *Eth. IV, xlvii.*   [10] *Eth. IV, lxiii.*   [11] *Eth. IV, lxxii.*

principle under the conditions of durational mutuality, its obligatoriness cannot be sustained. And in that case the phrase 'as much as possible' must be interpreted as meaning 'as much as mutuality demands'; and I think that Spinoza's text bears this interpretation. He means 'as much as possible without sacrificing the principle'. 'I say *as much as possible*; for although men are ignorant, they are nevertheless men who, when we are in straits, are able to afford us human assistance—the best we can receive.'[1] Here what is in question is the acceptance of favours from the ignorant, and the solution is that though refusal is the 'exemplary' dictate of reason, yet it is contrary to reason, under the conditions of mutuality, to make enemies by such refusal.

1. *Mutuality*

In the example just cited the fundamental dictate of reason is conceived as self-preservation by every means of self-improvement. We have already touched upon the common criticism of Spinoza's ethics, based on this, that it is fundamentally egoistic, and rejected its ethical import;[2] but the criticism is less easily disposed of in the inverse form that his application of 'exemplary' principle under the conditions of human mutuality is sometimes too exclusively centred on the emendation of the self, and takes too little account of the special needs of the hostile other. The instance of Spinoza's unqualified exclusion of hatred from the dispositions of the man who is guided by reason has already been mentioned,[3] and the inference from the proposition 'hatred can be destroyed by love'[4] to the conclusion that 'he who lives according to the guidance of reason strives as much as possible to repay hatred . . . with love',[5] is, perhaps, hardly to be justified.[6] For hatred may well be increased by a response of love by reason of the absence of any sign that is adversely significant of resentment in the hated one—interpreted as pusillanimity or moral self-exaltation. Hatred can be exhausted by allowing it adequate satisfaction—though there is much to be said for the rational restraint of resentment.

---

[1] *Eth. IV, lxx, Sch.*   [2] See above, pp. 101–2.   [3] See above, p. 120.
[4] *Eth. III, xliii.*   [5] *Eth. IV, xlvi.*
[6] To hate the hatred, but love the hater, is not to love the hater *as such*. The distinction, therefore, only emphasizes the one I am making.

'Mutual ethics', then, must take due rational account, not only of self-improvement, but also of the disposition of the other with a view to his improvement, and it is failure to do this that constitutes moral priggery.

Spinoza himself is well aware of the general point I am emphasizing. Pity, e.g., finds no place in 'exemplary ethics' since *ex hypothesi* the self alone is at fault, and its presence is evil and unprofitable;[1] but nevertheless, though pity is apt to lead to foolish deeds, and may be awakened by deceit under conditions of mutuality, 'it is good in so far as it shows that a desire of living uprightly is present . . . just as pain is called good in so far as it shows that the injured part has not yet putrified'.[2] So again with humility, repentance, shame, hope, fear, etc., though they are not 'exemplary' virtues, but 'passions', they 'are productive of more profit than disadvantage' 'inasmuch as men seldom live as reason dictates'. 'It is not to be wondered at, therefore, that the prophets, thinking rather of the good of the community than of a few, should have commended so greatly humility, repentance, and reverence.'[3]

But though 'mutual ethics' may commend what 'exemplary ethics' excludes, these are not in principle opposed to one another, for the latter is the exposition under the conditions of distributive unilateral self-reference of the fundamental principles on which the former is framed. Thus, the more integral the community of men becomes, the nearer must 'mutual' and 'exemplary' ethics approximate, and conduct among true friends is rarely governed by the principles applicable in a pulverulent society; and in a pure 'state of nature' would be ruled by no principles of ethical mutuality. It is in the light of this distinction, and under the assumption of generally favourable social conditions, that we must read Spinoza's reflection that 'although men generally determine everything by their inclination, many more advantages arise from their common union. It is better, therefore, to endure with equanimity the injuries inflicted by them, and to apply our minds to those things which subserve concord and the

---

[1] *Eth. IV, l et Cor.* Note that it is the *pity* that is said to be bad, i.e. for the *pitying man.* But the rational effort for the alleviation of the object of pity is good, and even a compassionate effort to this end, however ill-directed, is to be preferred to its absence. For 'he who is moved neither by reason nor by pity to be of any service to others is properly called inhuman'.

[2] *Eth. IV, lviii, Sch.*   [3] *Eth. IV, liv, Sch.*

establishment of friendship.'[1] For true self-interest, which involves the true interest of the other, may demand obstruction to,
and even destruction of, the apparent interest of both other and
self, for the rational ordering of durational association in the
'common order of nature' cannot be simply identified with that
of the community of eternal finite beings in *Natura*, though the
realization of this is the norm to which all durational moralization must be asymptotic.

2. *Civility*

While all durational moralization must be conceived as approximation to the eternal community which is its unattainable ideal
upper limit, equally it may be regarded as a movement from an
ideal lower limit or 'state of nature'—an unemended state of distributive unilateral self-reference. This cannot be conceived in the
Hobbesian form of a war of all against all, for according to the
status of the finite agent in *Natura* his self-reference involves
more or less privation, more or less alienation from 'self, and
God, and things' (to use Spinoza's recurrent phrase). But in the
'state of nature' mutual hostility is at a maximum, and mutual
co-operation at a minimum. With man, e.g., the conditions of
birth and early nurture require co-operation, and in general,
since things which have nothing in common cannot be opposed, a
state of complete hostility, unlike one of complete co-operation,
cannot be conceived.

Nevertheless, the ideal lower limit of human emendation may
be regarded as an approximation to an impossible pure 'state of
nature' in which mutual hostility is universal—for at least it is
rampant among barbarian hordes conceived in the most primitive
form. Emergence from such a condition raises questions of great
philosophical importance which are crucial for Spinoza's political theory. How is the 'wolf-man' to be set upon the path of
moral self-emendation?

First let it be said that the historicity of a universal relative
'state of nature' among men is of no essential philosophical importance, for the same problems arise whenever there is danger
of wholly uncontrolled and unemended action among men. And
that danger is ubiquitous and continual.

---

[1] *Eth. IV, App.* xiv.

Though Spinoza does not distinguish the *human* 'state of nature, in which hostility is rampant from a *pure* 'state of nature' in which it is universal, this need not discredit his account of the 'philosophical history' of human development. For this is not to be thought of as a 'natural history', still less as a chronological history, of human society and culture, but has simultaneous and recurrent application, as focused upon the development of each individual and society in relation with its 'world', throughout that development, though more or less 'telescoped' by such emendation as may have been achieved. Indeed, his failure to do so renders the stages of that history more easily discernible, since it is plain that from a supposedly pure 'state of nature' there could be no escape by way of moral emendation, save in so far as it were so modified as to render human life tolerably enduring. A life 'nasty, brutish, and short' (or we should rather say 'empty, impotent, and momentary') affords no opportunity for improvement; and in so far as man's life approximates to such a state he is incapable of attaining moral status. The pulverulence of the 'state of nature' must first be overcome.

Now, mutual hostility not merely *divides* men, but it is only possible in so far as they share a common nature, pursue the same objects, lay claim to the same territory, etc. And in so far as their powers are also more or less equally matched, life itself must be brief and wretched, and moral culture impossible, unless some way is discovered by which their unemended efforts can be so limited and canalized as to be brought to tolerable unison. The so-called 'contract' by which civic order is established, and by which the many 'agree' to be subject to the will of one, or of few, sufficiently powerful to compel subservience to a common 'law' embodying that will, expresses the actual form of this way of life. Doubtless, in a pure 'state of nature' such a discovery would (like that 'state' itself) be impossible, but in the *human* 'state of nature' it is easy to find its source in the family which is the *sine qua non* of human birth and early nurture, which naturally develops towards the genetically interrelated and interdependent tribe of blood-relations. However that may be (and it is not investigated by Spinoza), it is by the establishment of such a 'contract' that enduring life is made possible for the individuals, so that moral culture can be pursued. But it is not itself a step in moral culture: it does but 'canalize', not emend, the natural

K

desires and efforts of self-referent individuals. They pursue the same objects, and lay claim to the same territory, but now under such limitations as render the pursuit and the claim capable of being as successful as the ineluctable conditions of human aggregation permit. Whereas in the 'state of nature' effort must be mostly futile, in the 'civic state' where a common 'law' is supported by sanctions (i.e. by appeal to the *passions* of men) limited success is assured. But so far as civic order *as such* is concerned the passions of men remain unemended. Civility is the *sine qua non* of morality, not its inchoation.

This, again, is not to say that any human aggregation can be found, or even conceived, in which there is nothing of the nature of moral development, but civic order under a common 'law' alone —certainly not among men (necessarily born and nurtured in the family): we are considering, not the natural history of human development, but its philosophical history or etiology.

Turning next to Spinoza's explicit doctrine concerning the 'state of nature' prior to the civic order that limits and canalizes it, we find that he claims that there is nothing evil or irrational in man's barbarous conduct in such a state. It is governed by no laws save the natural right of every being to maintain itself, i.e. to exert its *conatus*, by all available means. For indeed, so far as it is positive, 'the power whereby natural beings exist and operate is the very power of God himself', and just as God's right is 'nothing else but his very power', i.e. his self-expressing active essence, 'every natural being has by nature as much right as it has power to exist and operate.'[1] It is rational for the barbarian living among barbarians so to act as to satisfy his desires, i.e. to preserve his being, and improve it, in the only way that he knows, and therefore can—just as it would be rational for a civilized, or even a morally cultivated, man cast among barbarians so to do in so far as morality and civility are of no avail. Under an established civic order, however, such actions are irrational and *naturally* evil[2] since the barbarian is thus in danger of the sanctions of the law sufficient to offset any advantage illegally ensued. In the 'civic

[1] *Tract. Polit. II, iii.*
[2] '*Naturally* evil' because contrary to self-preservation. For there is a 'pseudo-morality' even in the 'state of nature', and the barbarian in that state who fails, e.g., by reason of sloth, to exert his best endeavours after self-preservation is 'naturally' bad. But this in no way qualifies, but rather emphasizes, the distinction drawn between morality and civility.

state' what is *naturally* good and rational for the subject is subjection to the common 'law' in the fulfilment of desire; what is
naturally good and rational for the ruler is control of the subjects,
i.e. what is within his power *vis-à-vis* the subjects, and will promote
due subjection in them. And so far as this is accomplished the civic
right of the subject is his power to pursue his own profit within
the 'law', and to set barriers to the despotic will of the ruler; and
the civic right of the ruler is to require the subjection of the subjects under a law so framed as to be capable of ensuring this in
view of the actual natures of the subjects.

But it must be remembered that we have here but the bare
skeleton of the minimum civic State unenlightened by the moral
culture of rulers and subjects made available by its foundation.
Its moralization remains to be considered; nevertheless, it is on
this foundation that all improvements of civic order, and all
moral culture dependent upon it, are framed, so that degenera-
tion in this will mar, and in the end destroy, the fairest State.

CHAPTER XI

THE CIVIC STATE AND MORALITY

Fundamentally, civility is a 'device'[1] by which the 'state of nature' is rendered effective without transcendence of the reign of the passions among men; yet it is profitable to men, not merely as facilitating the satisfaction of the passions by their ordered self-limitation and canalization, but chiefly as providing a rampart of mutual security within which that truer profit which morality pursues may be achieved and enhanced. By civility the pulverulence of distributive unilateral self-reference is compacted by the harnessing of the conflicting passions for their own satisfaction—the sanctions of the law being effective as utilizing the passions of fear and hope for such moderation of mutually hostile endeavours as will facilitate the limited satisfaction of individuals' desires which, otherwise, can find none—or only the briefest. For government without sanctions, on the one hand, is a dream, neither reason nor religion serving to render them superfluous: they who 'persuade themselves that the multitude . . . can ever be induced to live according to the bare dictate of reason, must be dreaming of the golden age of the poets, or of a stage-play';[2] and though religion teaches a better way, 'it has too little power over the passions, availing in the hour of death, when disease has subdued them, and the man lies prone, or in temples where men do no business, but least of all where it is most needed, in the market-place or the palace'.[3] On the other hand, 'that a dominion may be permanent, its affairs must be so ordered that those who administer them, whether led by reason or by passions, cannot be induced to act in bad faith or basely', for 'the virtue of a dominion is its security'.[4] Thus, neither good nature nor mere unbridled force in the rulers, neither mere slavishness nor mere impotence in the subjects, will serve for

---

[1] The term is John Laird's: see *The Device of Government*, Cambridge, 1945, in which its use is well-defended in Ch. I.

[2] *Tract. Polit.*, i, 5.   [3] *Loc. cit.*

[4] *Op. cit.*, i, 6. The rulers, *qua* rulers, are not subject to the sanctions of the law; nevertheless, the sanction of dethronement always threatens them.

security and permanence. Both rulers and subjects 'are of necessity subject to the passions', to envy, vengeance, pity, and the like, which are sources of disagreement, and seek to enforce agreement with their own desires among all.[1] Thus what is above all requisite is a balance of limited and canalized powers, on the one hand rightly to govern, and on the other rightly to submit[2]— 'right' government and 'right' submission each involving adaptation to the powers and status of the other party.

So far we have spoken, in the main, of the most primitive and essential form of civility, the principles of which can never be wholly superseded without peril to the State, in view of the distributive character of individual unilateral self-reference. There is, and can be, no State that is not in danger from the barbarian that lurks beneath the veneer of civility and pseudo-morality in every man. Nevertheless, developed expressions of civility cannot remain wholly unmodified by the achievement and enhancement of morality as it is developed *passim* within its rampart; and the theory of the State must take due account of this—yet without thereby superseding its radical essence and principles. For however it may be moralized, the State remains at root but a durational 'device', and not, like the finite individual, an efflux of *Natura*; and its principles, therefore, cannot be deduced from those of a 'city of God', i.e. from perfect human community in *Natura naturata*.

I. THE CIVIC STATE

So far we have sought to isolate the radical essence of civility as the *sine qua non* among aggregated men of all moral development. We are not concerned in our 'philosophical history' of human

[1] *Tract. Polit.*, i. 5.

[2] Cf. *Tract. Polit.*, vii, 30, concerning the refusal of Ferdinand of Castile to deprive the Arragonese of their established rights after their kingdom had fallen to him by inheritance: 'Not yet being accustomed to absolute dominion, he dared to make no such attempt, but replied thus to his counsellors: that not only had he received the kingdom of Arragon on those terms, and most solemnly sworn to observe them, and not only was it barbarous to break faith, but he was assured that his kingdom would be stable as long as concern for security was no greater in the king than in the subjects, so that neither the king should outweigh the subjects, nor yet the subjects the king; for if either party were too powerful, the weaker would not only try to recover its former equality, but in vexation at its injury to retaliate against the other, whence would follow the ruin of either or both. Which very wise words I could not enough wonder at had they proceeded from a king accustomed to rule, not free men, but slaves.'

development with the question of the actual occurrence of such a primordial civility limiting and canalizing the natural rights of individuals, any more than with the similar question concerning the prior 'state of nature'. In any case, by its very nature it would be evanescent, seeing that by it moral development is made possible under the microcosmic *nisus* that more or less privatively characterizes man as self-referent finite of middle status in *Natura*. As durationally actual, therefore, civility is always permeated with morality of greater or less perfection—permeated, but not superseded. Further, by reason of nature or circumstance the moral development of the individuals is unequal, so that the permeation of civility by morality will vary from man to man and from society to society, and will at best be limited since 'all men are born ignorant, and before they can learn the right way of life, even if they have been well brought up, and acquire the habit of virtue, the greater part of their life has passed away', so that 'in the meanwhile they are bound to live and preserve themselves as far as they can by the unaided impulses of desire'.[1] Yet the State must cater for all classes of men, whether subjects or rulers.

1. *Its Absolute Civic Right*

Now, the essence of the civil 'contract' is the subordination of subjects to rulers, so that in the civic state, the right of the ruler, *qua* ruler, over the subject, *qua* subject, is absolute. Yet this absolute right lies in the power of the ruler, which stems from that of the subjects in so far as they are faithful to the 'contract', finding their highest profit under civic order, i.e. the rule of the government as in *their* interest. Thus, even where all are ruled by passion, the subject is no slave, save in so far as, by dissentience, he enslaves himself, i.e. is by nature a slave to his passions, and not merely subject to them. The civilized man, even though subject to passions, and ruled by them, knows a better way of satisfying them. Thus civic sanctions affect only the barbarians, for subjection to the civic law ensures avoidance of the sanctions, and security for permitted passions. Nor are these principles fundamentally changed by the permeation of civility by morality, though now subjection develops from submission motivated by

---

[1] *Tract. Theo.-Pol.*, *xvi.*

fear and hope to 'obedience' motivated by veneration for the law or its promulgator, and dissentience from barbarism to wickedness. If all men were civilized, and all civilized men good, the State as such would be redundant, and men would only need to be taught what is expedient or what is truly good. The latency of barbarism, and the liability of men to wickedness require that the civic right and power of the State be absolute, i.e. that its subjects should be properly subordinate to its rulers.

But this in no way conflicts with what has been said about the due balance of the powers of subjects and rulers: the power of the rulers must be sufficient to ensure the subjection of the subjects; and the power of the subjects sufficient to require from the rulers an order that will ensure security for the satisfaction of desires thus canalized or moralized. For failure on either side must tend towards reversion to the 'state of nature'. This balance of powers, however, need not be secured merely by the exercise of extrinsic power of rulers over subjects, and of subjects over rulers; and as morality develops within the rampart of civility, the powers of rulers over subjects and of subjects over rulers become more and more intrinsic or rational—rulers finding that their true interest lies in that of their subjects, and subjects that their true interest lies in willing obedience. Indeed, this is not a transition from mere force in the rulers to rational leadership, and from mere dissentience in the subject, threatening rebellion, to willing obedience, for even a master must take the measure of his slaves, and the rebellious slaves of their master—for the opposing powers are relative. Nevertheless, the transition from compulsion to benefaction in the rulers, and from submission to 'obedience' in the subjects, is no mere change of emphasis, but a real permeation of civility by morality, involving an enhancement both of individual freedom in the obedient subject, and also of the absolute right and power of the government. That subject is most free who is 'obedient' rather than submissive to the law; and that State is most effective which depends least on the subjects' submissiveness, and most on their 'obedience'. Thus, the absolute right and power of the State is no mere dogma or superstition under which men must be subdued, but the principle necessarily embodied in every State in so far as it is a 'State', and not a crumbling edifice of irrational expediencies or brutalities.

These conditions are realized in so far as rulers govern in

accordance with what reason prescribes under the conditions set
by the actual natures of the subjects; and in so far as subjects, in
the greatest number, or most influential part, obey in virtue of
their recognition of the rationality of the laws. That is, since men
are motivated by *affectus* rather than pure reason, what is most
favourable to the State as a human 'device' is that love joined with
astonishment at the wisdom of the rulers and their laws which we
call 'veneration'[1] among the subjects, and the 'exertions' of
'strength of mind' and 'magnanimity' in the rulers, rather than
pride, ferocity, lust, avarice, and the like passions, for the maintenance of veneration among the well-disposed, of fear and hope
among the indifferent, and of consternation among would-be
dissentients.[2]

Turning briefly from the internal to the external relations of
States, it should be noted that in Spinoza's view, apart from the
existence of treaties and contracts so arranged as to be, on
balance, in the interest of all parties, and thus sanctioned by their
otherwise opposing powers, civic States exist and operate as in a
'state of nature', i.e. under the law of nature that each pursues its
own interest, bad faith not being excluded. Contracts and treaties,
therefore, may be regarded as constituting a sort of pseudo-
civility of States under which 'law' has no central source, and
sanctions are distributively imposed—a state which may be
compared with a stage in the development of tribal civility
preparatory for that which, as Collingwood has reminded us, held
sway in the societies portrayed in the northern sagas. Some
development of international order, may perhaps, be discerned
since Spinoza's epoch, but not such as to discredit his analysis.
Thus the absolute right and power of the State in external affairs
is modified only in so far as *international* civility is established—
and, of course, generally permeated by the morality developed
within the member-States under the *aegis* of their internal civility.

----

[1] *Eth. III, lii, Sch.*

[2] Since our interest is in principles rather than examples, we need not spend
time here in considering the special ways in which these conditions may be
instituted and corroborated in the several kinds of polity considered by Spinoza
(viz. *monarchical*, in which one man, supported by his chosen generals, counsellors, and friends, is ruler: *aristocratic*, in which patricians form the supreme
authority, and are *elected* by the authority itself; and *democratic*, in which all
qualified citizens exercise dominion, i.e. are *not elected*, but *destined* to govern
by reason of age, primogeniture, wealth, sex, allegiance, independence, etc.).
These topics occupy the greater part of the *Tractatus Politicus*.

2. *The Limits of Its Power*

But much more must be said about the internal relations of the civic State. It is often too readily assumed that to contend that the State has absolute right or power is to imply that it can do no wrong—a proposition that is certainly rejected by Spinoza. It is true that the State cannot be convicted of crime under its own laws, nor can its rulers, *qua* rulers, be said to do wrong in the sense that the subjects, *qua* subjects, do wrong by neglect or breach of the laws. Nevertheless, just as in the 'state of nature' there can be no crime, because there is no civic law, yet the barbarian does wrong in so far as by indolence or cowardice he fails to exert his utmost strength to preserve his life, so with the rulers of the State, though as rulers they are above their own laws, they do wrong in so far as by their actions they weaken or bring into contempt their own authority. And this they do in so far as they not merely rule too little, but attempt to rule too much, i.e. assume a power which is beyond their scope save as parasitical upon their proper power which is thereby weakened. Just as the barbarian in the 'state of nature' wrongs himself by indolence in the pursuit of self-preservation, so that State does wrong when it weakens itself either by attempting to do what is impossible (e.g. to govern men's minds), what brings it into peril of dissolulution (e.g. to limit unduly freedom of speech), or even what is likely to arouse indignation by undue interference in matters of individual behaviour. 'He who seeks to regulate everything by law is more likely to arouse vices than to reform them. It is better to grant what cannot be abolished, even though it be in itself harmful.'[1] These are not limitations of the absolute civic right of the State, but of the scope of that right or power: 'He who holds dominion is not bound to observe the terms of the contract by any cause other than that which bids a man in the state of nature to beware of being his own enemy, lest he should destroy himself.'[2]

Thus, the State is both absolute in power or right, and also limited in its scope, and without contradiction, for the one cannot be maintained without the other, the absolute power being destroyed by diversion beyond its proper range.

Now the prime mission of the State is to constitute a 'rampart'

[1] *Tract. Theo.-Pol.*, xx. [2] *Tract. Polit.*, iv, 6.

within which, among other forms of culture, morality may be developed; and though morality, too, makes for security, its end is not merely this, but emendation. Thus, though morality in the actual State more or less *permeates* civility, it cannot by civility be governed or limited. Moral duty includes the welfare of the civic State (as its *sine qua non*), but extends far beyond it. So again, intellectual, aesthetic, and religious culture, rightly pursued, cannot endanger security (without which their pursuit is impossible or brief), but their proper ends transcend this. The State, therefore, as by these forms of culture permeated, must protect, and may nurture, but must not seek to control or limit their essential pursuit—for the emancipation and protection of which, indeed, it exists.

Such is the essential tenor of Spinoza's celebrated plea for the 'liberty of thought and speech' in the *Tractatus Theologico-Politicus* 'in which it is set forth that freedom of thought and speech not only may, without prejudice to piety and the public peace, be granted; but also may not, without danger to piety and the public peace, be withheld'. That the precise limits of civic control are difficult to set, and relative to human nature and condition, is obvious enough from Spinoza's own discussion. For example, if we compare his recommendations concerning religion and secular thought, we find that though inward religion and private thought are beyond State-control, the outward rites and observances of religion fall within it, while the outward expression of thought in speech ought in general to be beyond it. And his reason seems to be that great weight is attached in the popular mind to spiritual authorities: 'everyone hangs on the lips, as it were, of those who possess it. We may even say that those who wield such authority have the most complete sway over the popular mind'[1]—whereas only 'agitators and rebels', who certainly ought to be controlled, can do much harm by speech; and 'he who disapproves of a law, and submits his judgement to the authorities, but does not break that law, deserves well of the State'.[2] These are reasons varying in weight from time to time, and even with speech, that of an influential public figure can hardly be judged by the same criterion as that of an obscure private citizen. But the general principle is clear enough: 'the dominion, to maintain its independence, is bound to preserve the causes of fear and reverence, otherwise

[1] *Tract. Theo.-Pol.*, xix.   [2] *O . cit.*, xx.

it ceases to be a dominion';[1] and this has application, not only to the actions of the subjects *vis-à-vis* the law, but also to those of the rulers as men holding authority, who must, in their private lives, uphold the majesty of the State with a standard of conduct even higher than is tolerable among obscure subjects.[2]

And finally, in the actual State, permeated by morality, particular care must be taken that general controls, defencible against the vicious, do not cause such offence to the virtuous as to do more harm on the one hand than good on the other: e.g. 'the more rulers strive to curtail freedom of speech, the more obstinately they are resisted—not, indeed, by the avaricious, by flatterers, and other simpletons who think that the greatest well-being lies in filling their stomachs and gloating over their moneybags, but by those whom good training, sound morality, and virtue have emancipated'.[3]

II. MODES OF MORALITY

In the actual civic State, as permeated by morality, true citizenship lies in obedience to laws regarded as just, and submission even to those regarded as unjust; and barbarism survives as outward conformity to the laws as a *pis aller*, a way of avoiding sanctions. In fact but few examples either of true citizenship or of mere barbarism are to be found; for the former requires a veneration for the laws, both to justify obedience and to induce submission to unjust laws the existence of which tends to its destruction; and the latter has in the main been superseded. The more or less bad citizen is thus by far the most common. Now mere outward conformity to the laws of the State to escape punishment, in so far as it becomes a way of life, may be regarded as a sort of *pseudo-morality*, just as the habit of obedience to the laws from veneration is a species of *dogmatic morality*. But neither pseudo-morality nor dogmatic morality is confined to man's relation to the civic laws; for the sanctions of society, and the veneration of authority, extend far beyond the specifically civic range. Nor again is dogmatic morality its highest expression, for this stems rather from rational insight than from external authority. Let us, then, consider these modes more generally.

---

[1] *Tract. Polit.*, iv, 4. [2] *Loc. cit.* [3] *Tract. Theo.-Pol.*, xx.

1. *Pseudo-Morality: Passion and Sanction*

Civility, as such, though it introduces outward order into the 'state of nature', necessitates no change, in subject or ruler, of man's natural subjection to his passions; it does but facilitate such a change. It operates non-morally by the imposition of sanctions: those of the law awakening fear in the subjects; those of secure power awakening hope in the rulers. It limits or extends, but not as such emends, the *affectus* of its members. Thus it is the *sine qua non* of moral culture, not its inchoation; its order is external, not internal, and it requires submission, and not 'obedience', in the subjects, mastery, not moral authority, in the rulers. And though such a pure unmoralized civic state, like the 'state of nature', would be hard to find, actions thus motivated are too common to need exemplification, whether in the political or in the moral sphere. Indeed, since the requirements of civic order (the establishment of peace and security) are generally in agreement with those of the emergent moral order (for which they are the *sine quibus non*) exemplification is hardly possible. It remains a moot point to the candid citizen how far he pays his taxes, e.g. from moral or purely civic motives, or how far he labours from cultural interest or for extrinsic reward—save where one or other motive is wholly excluded (as it can rarely be under every disguise). And though the civic motive is thus in essence non-moral, it may be described as 'pseudo-moral' in so far as it favours action that facilitates moral development in others (by removing obstruction) and in the self (by tending to the formation of a habit of deliberation). And the same principles apply to actions which lie beyond the civic sphere, where the sanctions are social rather than legal, and tend to produce outward conformity to custom or fashion rather than inward conviction.

Many have thought that such pseudo-morality is all that the metaphysical principles of Spinoza can rightly support—an error which is easily traced to a fundamental misunderstanding of those principles. We have now to examine Spinoza's account of the moral life, and its development, among the unintellectual many and the more enlightened few.

2. *Dogmatic Morality: Veneration and 'Obedience'*

The establishment of civic order opens the way to moral development in both subjects and rulers, and this development reciprocally permeates the civic order with morality. For mere mastery and submission there is increasingly substituted civic authority and 'obedience' under moralization—but not to the exclusion of the former where morality has not permeated. 'It is the fact of submission, not the reason for submitting, that makes a subject', yet 'obedience has regard not so much to the external, as to the internal, action of the mind; so that he is most under the dominion of another who with his whole mind resolves to submit to all his commands; and it follows that he holds the greatest dominion who reigns over the minds of his subjects.'[1] In so far as civility is moralized, civic action is no mere *pis aller*, but a way of true profit, and the decrees of the ruler gain *moral* force. The moral right of the ruler emerges only with respect to subjects who hold him in veneration by reason of his wisdom, his majesty, his hereditary status, or some special character.

But morality is not confined to the civic sphere; and the same principles have application wherever outstanding individuals are able to impress their fellows as unusually wise, or saintly, or in some way morally unique—as for example the prophets of ancient Israel about which Spinoza has so much to say in the *Tractatus Theologico-Politicus*. These were not primarily foretellers of future events, but interpreters of the mind and will of God as imaginationally conceived or 'revealed'. They excelled in the power of 'free imagination'[2] devoted to moral ends, and not in intellectual power—these diverse powers being commonly opposed. The interpretations of the prophets were thus mainly allegorical in form, and coloured by their private opinions; so that their authority was moral rather than intellectual—and that only in so far as their minds were devoted to what is right and good. The moral authority of a prophet over his hearers sprang from his self-assurance of divine mission arising from the vividness of his imagination of the nature and will of God (this often being given the form of some 'sign' or vision), and the veneration evoked in his hearers by reason of his devout life (rather than his cultivated intellect). The prophet, therefore, would more

[1] *Tract. Theo.-Pol.*, xvii.   [2] See above, Chapter VII, section iii.

correctly be styled a '*Gottvertrunkener Mann*' than was Spinoza himself (essentially a man of intellect) by Novalis—indeed, the prophet was often a simple uneducated countryman.

Where civic morality is dogmatic, then, as requiring 'obedience' to the decrees of the ruler, morality in general is dogmatic as requiring 'obedience' to commandments 'revealed' to venerable human authorities, i.e. *morally* venerable. Yet, of course, sophists have often been taken as moral authorities; veneration may be misplaced, and true moral authority is essentially rooted, not in the extrinsic man who interprets the requirements of virtue, but in the obedient moral agent himself—his veneration reflecting an inward *nisus* to virtue.[1] And it is in virtue of this that dogmatic morality involves the substitution of 'exertions' for passions as the proper motives of human endeavour.

Those who have objected to Spinoza's ethical doctrine, therefore, that in it no place is found for the essentially moral conception of 'duty'[2] can have read the *Tractatus Theologico-Politicus* to little purpose, allowing the rational elucidation of the *Ethics* to occupy the whole range of his ethical teaching (and interpreting that as a sort of ethical naturalism—the acquirement of virtue as a happy accident, and its continuance a fateful necessity or impossibility). But common human morality is mainly dogmatic, and for this what is essential is obedience to commandment, rather than clear knowledge of its rational foundation; nor is the obvious danger of dogmatic morality (viz. misplaced veneration) so great as it might seem, for men are less prone to venerate the vicious 'prophet' than to be misled intellectually by the sophist; and 'a man is rightly said to believe morally or immorally in so far as he is moved to obedience by his opinions, or from them assumes licence to sin or rebel. Thus if any man by believing what is true becomes rebellious, his belief is immoral, and if, on the contrary, by believing what is false he becomes obedient, his belief is moral. For true knowledge of God, we have shown, is not commanded, but is a divine gift.'[3]

---

[1] Cf. 'Even the Holy One of the Gospels must first be compared with our ideal of moral perfection before we can recognize him as such' (Kant, *Fundamental Principles*, § 2).

[2] E.g. A. E. Taylor, 'Some Inconsistencies in Spinozism' (*Mind*, N.S. xlvi, p. 291).

[3] *Tract. Theo.-Pol., xiii.*

3. *Essential Morality:* Affectus *and Truth*

Apart from the danger of misplaced veneration, the most notable defect of dogmatic morality has always been felt to be its capacity to involve men in conflicting duties, arising chiefly from the diversity of venerated authorities. This defect can only be satisfactorily met by a critique of authorities in the light of the source of all moral authority. For example, where loyalty to my neighbour conflicts with loyalty to the State, each of which is commanded, the conflict can only be resolved by rational inquiry into the status and scope of the diverse commanding authorities. 'It is certain that loyalty to his fatherland is the highest that any man can maintain, for with the overthrow of the State nothing good can stand, but all comes into confusion, and only wrath and the greatest licence reign, with universal terror. Whence it follows that nothing can be held to be a duty to one's neighbour which is not wrong if there follows thence injury to the whole State; and on the contrary, there is nothing disloyal to him which may not be attributed to duty, if it is done for the sake of the preservation of the State.'[1] It is reason applied to the conditions of the durational life of aggregated men that subordinates all private and social duties, whatever may be the elevation commonly accorded to their promulgators, to civic loyalty. Thus, he continues: 'It is right to give up my coat also to him who contends with me and wishes to seize my cloak; but where it is judged that this is a danger to the preservation of the State, it is my duty, on the contrary, to call him to judgement even if he may be condemned to death.'[2] This is but a limiting example, indeed, of that right application of 'exemplary ethics' under the conditions of mutuality that I have called 'mutual ethics'; and just as the requirements of mutuality cannot be rightly estimated save in the light of knowledge of the metaphysical status of durational agents, their relations with *Natura*, and the means of their rehabilitation from multiplex unilateral self-reference to 'reference to God', so also the supremacy, *sub specie durationis*, of civic duty

---

[1] *Tract. Theo.-Pol.*, *xix.*

[2] *Op. cit.*, xix. It is said that Spinoza himself, on the death of his father, defended his inheritance in the courts against the unjust claims of his sister; but, having won his case, conceded the goods to her; thus fulfilling both his civic and his moral duties. Such a happy solution, however, is not often available.

over private and social duty can only be certified on the foundation of true knowledge of the human predicament. For it is by
no means assured by durational experience, which rather
suggests that the harm to the State being small relative to
that suffered by one's neighbour, it is the latter that should be
avoided as being the greater evil. But this is to have resort to
expediency—and in spite of the fact that moralists are prone to
argue, on the contrary, that the superiority of moral to civil
principle *de jure* should imply its universal supremacy *de facto*,
so that to judge otherwise is to fall back on mere expediency. But
just as 'mutual ethics' is not an ethics of compromise or expediency, so also the maintenance of civility where it conflicts with
private and social morality is a genuine obligation because in the
human predicament of multiplex unilateral self-reference civility
is the *sine qua non* of all emendation.

The principles of essential morality, therefore, by which the
moral duties promulgated by venerated authorities must be critically ordered have an intellectual foundation in adequate knowledge of man's status and predicament, so that the true profit of
the individual is to be sought in knowledge of 'himself and God
and things.'

Essential morality, however, must not be conceived as limited
to such arbitration between conflicting dogmatic duties: its principles are of radical import and universal application. The manner in which intellect is morally effective is explained in the
opening propositions of *Ethices V*, following hard upon the rejection, in the *Preface* to this *Part*, of Descartes's doctrine of the
unlimited power of the human will over the passions. In *Ethices
IV, vii*, Spinoza had denied that any *affectus* can be extinguished
or restrained save by an opposing stronger *affectus*—a principle
that might well seem, *prima facie*, to deprive the intellect of all
moral power. But plainly, Spinoza himself drew no such conclusion, and we must next consider how, according to him, the
intellect is morally effective, and what is that 'power of the intellect' which, as the title of *Part V* suggests, constitutes 'human
liberty'.

Broadly speaking (for the merest sketch must suffice) the position of Spinoza is as follows: the mind is essentially the idea of
the body, i.e. of extended nature as microcosmically expressed—
the body thus being in eternal community with extended nature

so far as, being finite, it can be. Under self-reference this community suffers privation, and the durational mind is the idea of the durational body as 'affected' by other durational bodies, i.e. it is the idea of the *affectiones* which confuse the natures of the 'affected' body and of the bodies by which it is 'affected'. The changes in these *affectiones* are such as to increase or diminish the perfection of the durational body, and thus also of the durational mind, and the ideas of these transitions are the *affectus* of joy, sadness, and desire. These are the primary *affectus* from which all mental dispositions are derived by association with ideas, more or less inadequate, of their supposed causes. In so far as these causes are extrinsic, and their causality transeunt, the *affectus* are passive, i.e. *passions*; in so far as they are intrinsic, and their causality immanent, they are active, i.e. '*exertions*'. Now morality consists in the restraint or extinction of the passions by 'exertions' or more generally, in the transformation of passions into 'exertions', or the substitution of 'exertions' for passions; and the moral power of the intellect lies in its effectiveness to this end.

Yet, no idea merely as *true* can have any power to restrain or extinguish passion:[1] it is not as truth that knowledge controls the passions, but as involving emendation of the understanding, i.e. the passage to a greater perfection which is an active *affectus* or 'exertion'. And this moral power is actualized in many forms and degrees. For example, it may arise from the nature of the derivative *affectus* as associations of primary *affectus* with ideas of their supposed causes: for increase of knowledge may result in a changed association, as when one's hatred for a man is extinguished by knowledge that he is not the cause of one's sadness, or that he acted under compulsion, or unwittingly. But here it would seem that the original *affectus* remains unchanged though associated with a different object as cause. And this can hardly be called the restraint or extinction of passion in any important ethical sense. The moral effectiveness of intellect must centre in its power to correct our 'knowledge of good or evil', i.e. our primary *affectus*: it must be capable of rendering that which is naturally a source of joy, morally a source of sadness, that which is naturally an object of desire, morally an object of

---

[1] *Eth. IV, vii.* Even the 'knowledge of good or evil' is effective, not by reason of its truth, but because it is an *affectus*, viz. a desire or aversion (for we call 'good' that which we desire).

L

aversion, or *vice versa*. This, of course, is impossible under unemended self-reference,[1] but morality stems essentially from the
'emendation of the intellect' made possible by the limitation of
the privation suffered by the finite being under self-reference
according to its microcosmic status.[2] The power of the intellect
lies therefore in the recognition of an *exemplar*, a self as emended
towards greater harmony with its undefected roots, a moral
nature with its own primary *affectus*, with a truer 'knowledge of
good or evil', *affectus* capable of opposing the natural passions,
and thus of restraining or extinguishing them *if they are weaker*.
For the moral power of the intellect is not absolute, but may itself
be restrained or extinguished by more vigorous natural passion.[3]
Yet the rational *affectus* or 'exertions' enjoy certain advantages
over the passions: 'The *affectus* which spring from, or are excited
by, reason are more powerful, if time be taken into account, than
those which relate to particular things which we contemplate as
absent';[4] also the causes of rational *affectus* are more consistent
and widespread than those of the passions,[5] so that their powers,
even if taken singly they are weaker than those of the passions
associated with a present cause, are firmer, and may thus be more
effective, especially as facilitating self-emendation in periods of
leisure from the more urgent passions.

All this implies no absolute durational power in the intellect
(which Spinoza denies), but equally it implies that in human life
the intellect is never morally impotent. And its power is aug-
mented with each movement towards self-emendation, or reference from self to God, and may receive aid from likeminded, or
more moralized, associates, as well as from reflection upon sure
dogmata in periods of tranquillity. For morality, though rooted
in man's partially undefected eternal nature, is no original gift of
durational nature, and it must be corroborated by self-cultivation
and mutual aid. Only the *nisus* is durationally given; the development is an *obligation* more or less vital as it bears more or less

---

[1] Though even here it finds its analogue, as when the sensation of pain,
normally a source of sadness, may become a source of joy when it is known to
give assurance of life in the painful member. As associated with this joy the
surgeon becomes an object of love, and not of hatred.

[2] For self-reference in *Natura naturata* as such involves no privation, in the
modus simplicissimus involves total privation, but in man, e.g. who stands
between these limits, involves only partial privation.

[3] *Eth. IV, xiv–xvii.*   [4] *Eth. V, vii.*   [5] *Eth. V, viii–xiii.*

essential reference to an eternal source and *exemplar*. Thus, the question remains: How far, and in what degrees and manners, is such an agent *free* in the actual resolution of his bifurcated potency, in the choice of good or evil? To this and allied questions we must finally turn our attention.

CHAPTER XII

THE FREE MAN

No part of Spinoza's doctrine—if it can be called a 'part': for as essentially activistic, the whole is a doctrine of freedom—has been so widely, and often so naïvely misunderstood and criticized as his account of human liberty. Usually his rejection of the common notion of freedom has been taken as a total denial of freedom itself. For this result anachronistic presuppositions concerning causation are mainly responsible, and its naïvety lies in the critics' failure to turn their attention to these. Great acuity is not required to infer that if 'causation' is essentially a sort of impulsion *a tergo*, and everything has its determinate 'cause', freedom is impossible, and where it is imagined to operate it is an illusion due to ignorance of the 'causes'. 'Men are deceived in that they suppose themselves to be free, which opinion is founded on this alone, that they are conscious of their actions, and ignorant of the causes by which they are determined.'[1] But the deception lies, not in the claim to be free, but in the false idea of what freedom is: '*Their idea* of freedom, therefore, is that they know no causes of their actions,'[2] and not discerning these, they deny all causal action. Thus they take freedom to mean uncaused action which, as we have seen, is for Spinoza a contradiction in terms—'action' being the actualization of potency, and 'causation' potency-in-act, and not impulsion *a tergo*. On the other hand, 'action' being actualization of potency, it is essentially free. Freedom, in short, is to be contrasted, not with determination, but with bondage, and a man's action is free in so far as his deed actualizes his own intrinsic potency, and is so far bound as it also confusedly actualizes the extrinsic potency of another. I say 'also', for a man's deed cannot *merely* actualize the potency of another, so that his 'bondage' is extrinsic compulsion *simpliciter*—for then it would not be *his* deed. Just as falsity is parasitical on truth, and vice on virtue, so bondage is parasitical on freedom. And this applies universally: a thing can only be made to do that of which its nature is

[1] *Eth. II, xxxv, Sch.*   [2] *Loc. cit.* (My italics).

capable. A billiard ball cannot be made to eat grass, nor a mind
to set a body in motion by impact; so that when the ball is
made to rotate, or the mind to think, the *making* is not *mere*
compulsion.

Actions, however, vary in perfection of agency, and thus also
in perfection of freedom: *Deus sive Natura* alone is perfectly free
in the perfect action that is eternal creation; finite agents, as
derivative, i.e. created, are free only 'as referred to God', and thus
in perfect community with their complement; and durational
agents, whose action is *conatus*, are imperfectly free according to
their status. But to be wholly under compulsion is not to exist at
all. For to *exist* is to *act*.

I. LIBERTY, BONDAGE, AND INDETERMINISM

Liberty and bondage, then, are modes of determination, adequate
and inadequate, and to identify liberty with indeterminacy *sans
phrase,* and bondage with determination wholly *ab extra,* are not
merely erroneous, but unintelligible. An agent cannot be free if he
determines nothing, nor can he be in bondage if he is wholly determined by another: in either case he is a mere cipher. In so far
as we *act*, we are free; but in so far as our action is limited and
modalized by another, we are in bondage: 'I say that we act when
anything is done, within us or beyond us, of which we are the
adequate cause . . .; contrariwise, I say that we suffer when anything is done within us, or anything follows from our nature, of
which we are only the partial cause.'[1] And 'I call that an adequate
cause, the effect of which can be clearly and distinctly perceived
by means of the cause; on the other hand, I call that cause inadequate, or partial, the effect of which cannot be understood by
means of the cause alone.'[2] Thus freedom is adequate causality;
bondage, inadequate causality. The free agent actualizes its own
potency without let or hindrance; the bounden agent actualizes
its own potency under the limitations set by the potency of
another, so that there is a confusion of fragmented potencies in
which each suffers privation, but neither, while the agents persist,
destruction. Only the infinite *causa sui* is independently free; the
finite agent is free only in so far as it acts in community with its

[1] *Eth. III, Def. ii.*   [2] *Eth. III, Def. i.*

complement in *Natura*; and it is in bondage in so far as its acts are in part those of another.

When, therefore, Spinoza rejects the vulgar notion of freedom as indeterminacy, i.e. as action without a cause, and affirms that all things are causally determined to exist and act in a certain manner, he is not denying that actions are free; on the contrary, in his view 'action' is *essentially* free, though the degree, and the modality, of the freedom varies with the integrity of the agent. Creation is free *sans phrase*; finite agency is free community; but *conatus* is a privative 'projection' of finite agency under self-reference, and its freedom is limited and modalized accordingly, but not negated. For though, as *conatus*, it is always subject to extrinsic counter-*conatus*, this subjection or bondage is but a privation of freedom, not extrinsic compulsion. It is thus that by obedience to true *dogmata* its bondage may be loosened, and by the 'emendation of the intellect' set at liberty.

That this has not been understood by Spinoza's critics is due in the main to their failure to realize that by a 'cause' he does not mean an actuality or event antecedent to another actuality in a prior established time, and determining it by compulsion *a praeterito* (for in that case causation would necessarily exclude freedom); causation is *essentially* the actualization of potency, i.e. where the potency is infinite, creation, where it is finite and derivative, active community with its complement (and in either case eternal and immanent); but where, by reason of self-reference, the potency is partly alien, and the actuality privative, the causation thus being inadequate and transeunt, it is durational *conatus*. Thus, cause and effect are not successive in a prior established time; it is duration that is posterior to the inadequation of causality under finite self-reference, and is temporalized, i.e. metrically punctuated, by the fragmentation of the eternal community of finite causes congruent therewith. Transeunt causality is not mere extrinsic compulsion *a praeterito*, but the durational actualization of fragmented and confused potency-in-act *sub specie conatus*.

Hume's denial of 'power' in the 'cause' to produce the 'effect', interpreted as a denial that transeunt causality is such mere compulsion, would thus not have been rejected by Spinoza; but equally, interpreted, as it must be, as a denial of all power in the 'cause' to determine the 'effect', it would have seemed to him

incredible.[1] It is only as durationally actualizing its own privative potency-in-act under the conditions set by another, that an
actual existent can be conceived as a transeunt cause; and it is
only as the actuality of its own privative potency-in-act as modified by that of the 'cause', that an actual existent can be conceived
as the effect of that cause. Thus the effect of a transeunt cause is a
function of the natures of both, i.e. of the associated privative
potencies that it durationally actualizes. The effect of a blow from
a hammer depends on the vigour of the blow and also on the
resistance of the thing struck.[2]

Thus what we call a 'transeunt cause' is some existent actualizing a certain potency-in-act partly in its own existing nature
and partly in modifying the existing nature of another; and this
modification of the other is its 'transeunt effect'. It is inadequate
in that it is only the partial cause of this effect (which varies with
the nature of the other), and it is transeunt or durational in that
its potency is only partly actualized in its own existing nature, and
must seek proper fulfilment by the adaptation of the other to its

[1] This must be the correct interpretation since the denial is based on the
absence of a perception of 'power' among the other contents perceived (or 'perceptions' as Hume calls them)—the *data* of experience being by him confined
to such contents. This, however, is but a truncated empiricism: for nothing
can be more intrinsically 'empirical' than the powers which we actualize in our
deeds, e.g., our perceptual power in our perceptions; though, of course, potency-
in-act, whether adequate (and thus the source of eternal actuality), or inadequate, i.e. *conatus* or effort (and thus the source of durational actuality), is, itself,
as such, no actuality, save as actual*ized*, i.e. as immanent in the actual. Thus
the rejection of 'effort', e.g., on the ground that the *'sense* of effort' is but a
complex of organic sensations, is *nihil ad rem*. To deny the empirical reality of
the potency-in-act immanent in our deeds on the ground that it is not itself
an actual deed, and thus no *object* of perception, is a mere paradox.

[2] This is not, of course, denied by those who would reduce transeunt causality to a function of uniformities of sequence, since the causal 'factor' and that
of the effect are always abstracted from the 'irrelevant' other 'factors' of the
particular existents. But what is overlooked, or insufficiently regarded, is that
the uniformity of recurrence of transeunt causal sequences is thus a product of
the abstraction. For neither the particular existents nor their 'factors' ever
recur (for the 'factors' are not existents, and thus do not even *occur*). By 'recurrence' is meant the *occurrence* of a multiplicity of 'instances' of some abstract
universal; and abstract universals are, primarily at least, products (as Spinoza
says) of a failure of imaginational discernment, and not real factors in the constitution of their supposed 'instances', viz. particular existents. And though as
discernment sharpens, the first crude universals of *mera experientia* are emended,
if the emendation is governed by the search for uniformity (the defect of which
facilitates discernment), the reduction of causality in terms of uniformity,
though scientifically pragmatic, is philosophically sophistical.

own profit—an effort which is more or less impeded by the reciprocal effort of the other. The actuality of the transeunt cause is not, as with an adequate cause, eternal, but continuant or durational. In so far as the other is adapted through this effort to the profit of the self, its continuance is enhanced; in so far as the other resists such adaptation, its continuance is checked; and its actual duration, therefore, is determined by the changing ratio of its potency with that of the others, with which it must compete. And because the agent is finite, and the 'common order of nature' indefinitely potent, the duration of the agent is necessarily limited within the sempiternity of durational nature. For 'no particular being is given in nature, than which another more potent and stronger is not given, but whatever is given, there is given another more potent by which it can be destroyed'.[1]

We have seen that the self-reference by which the complement of the finite agent in *Natura* is alienated, only alienates it in part, according to his grade of finite perfection, so that every self-referent agent is in part eternal and in part durational; we can now say that it is thus that the actuality of the finite agent springs in part from its intrinsic potency, and so far is not subject to the intrinsic or the extrinsic limitations of duration, but is eternal; and in part its actuality springs from extrinsic potency and is durationally modified by that potency. And further, even that part which is durational may, by emendation be eternalized, or by indulgence durationally impaired (i.e. liberated by its own 'exertions', or further enslaved by its own passions), as well as corroborated or destroyed (or both in varying measure from birth and towards death) under the vicissitude of its durational destiny; for its actual duration is a function of the development or impoverishment of its own durational potency, and of the extrinsic potencies of the things with which it has to do.

II. DURATIONAL LIBERATION AND ITS MODES

Every being in any sense, or degree, or modality active (and only thus can it be said to be 'actual') is in that sense, degree, and modality free. Bondage is not the mere absence of freedom (for this is non-being), but its privation—a positive state parasitical on freedom. And liberation is liberation from bondage, not from

[1] *Eth. IV*, *Ax.*

non-being; the perfecting of durational being, not its origination. Here we are concerned with the self-liberation of the bounden durational agent, rather than with the accidental enfranchizement that comes from the change or destruction or removal of the alien object of passion, i.e. with *moral*, rather than with 'natural', liberation.

1. *'Free Choice'*

If all the deeds of an agent were, *per impossibile*, compelled, i.e. extrinsically determined *a praeterito*, moral self-liberation would be impossible; and if all were intrinsically determined by the potency of the self, i.e. the result of free necessity, it would be unnecessary. Self-liberation is a movement from subjection to another, mediated by passion, towards that community with the other which springs from self-mastery, and is mediated by 'exertion'. It is a passage from self-reference towards 'reference to God'. Such a passage is only possible in so far as the agent *chooses* between the alternatives of freedom and bondage, i.e. true and false freedom. Further, 'choice' *essentially* involves freedom, for an extrinsically determined 'alternative' is not a 'choice' at all. A compelled choice is a chimera.

Now, it will be said, and rightly, that Spinoza plainly denies that freedom means 'free decision',[1] and, indeed, on his principles 'free decision' is impossible since where there is perfect freedom (viz. unhindered actualization of potency) no decision is required; and where decision is required (as in choice) it is because potency is bifurcated, and thus hindered, so that freedom is limited or modalized. 'Free decision', therefore, taken *au pied de la lettre*, is a self-contradictory notion.

How, then, it will be asked, can decisive choice be in any sense, degree, or modality, free? The sting of the question lies, however, in the truncated conception of 'choice' as involving nothing but the isolation of one alternative by the elimination of the other, whereas in truth it involves *selection* and *rejection*, which are founded upon *valuation* and *preference*, which express the operant potency of the agent. In choice the agent cannot be indifferent or extrinsically coercive.

Thus, just as in all durational agency the agent is free in so

---

[1] *'Liberum decretum'*, see *Epist. lviii.*

far as, and in the manner in which, his deed is the actuality of
his intrinsic potency as conditioned by potency extrinsic (for
conatus, though subject to the confusion in *affectio* of intrinsic and
extrinsic potencies, is essentially distinct from extrinsic coercion),
so also in choice the agent is similarly free, since the preference
which, in the act, resolves the bifurcation of potency, is not independent of, but latent in, that bifurcation. For the bifurcation is
not dissociation, but arises from alternative reference to self more
or less emended, or reference to God. Potency, indeed, confers
a value on the deed, and this value emerges as a preference where
the potency is bifurcated. This, in choosing between deeds pos-
sibly actual the agent is actualizing his *elective potency*; and he is
more or less free in so far as, and in the manner in which, this
potency is intrinsically *his*, though more or less confusedly involved in potency extrinsic. As choosing, however, the agent
cannot be wholly in bondage (for bondage is parasitical on freedom), though he is more or less bound as his preference inclines
towards passion or towards 'exertion'.

I have already hinted that though in the act the valuation
Thus the decision is free only in the degree that pertains to the
modality of the action as a 'choice', i.e. it is neither a false freedom
of indifference, nor a perfect freedom of eternal self-actualization of potency-in-act, or free necessity. It is 'free choice', i.e.
choice that has the degree and modality of freedom proper to that
choice. And this will vary according to the truth or 'evidence' of
the valuations that are 'integrated' in the decision, and resolved in
the act.

I have already hinted that though in the act the valuation
or preference determines the act but does not resolve the bifurcation of the potency, the actualization of the choice does
modify the *sequent* bifurcation of potency—and this must
be emphasized. The choice of the truly better enhances the
preference for the truly good or better, whereas the choice
of the truly worse, i.e., the merely apparent better, enhances
the preference for the truly bad, i.e. the merely apparent good,
or for the truly worse, i.e. the merely apparent better. It is
thus that right choice tends to the durational establishment of
virtue, and wrong choice to the durational establishment of
vice.

So much for the general principles of elective freedom; let us
next consider the modes in which it is durationally actualized

under the conditions of finite mutuality or subordination, corresponding with the distinction of essential and dogmatic morality.[1]

2. *Free Submission or 'Obedience'*

The distinction between 'submission' and 'obedience' has already been emphasized[2]—especially as that between the attitude of the good citizen towards the civic laws, and their promulgators, and that of the bad citizen, in the partly moralized civic State. As Spinoza says: though 'it is the fact of submission, and not the reason for submission, that makes a subject', yet 'obedience has regard, not so much to the external, as to the internal, action of the mind'. 'He holds the greatest dominion who reigns over the minds of his subjects.'[3] So also with submission to the moral import of the 'prophetic' imaginations: obedience to prophetic *dogmata* means not mere submission, but the resolution 'with one's whole mind to submit' to the commands of a venerated authority. Obedience is *free* submission.

But in what sense and degree can submission be free? That the question is closely associated with the parallel question, already considered,[4] as to how imagination can be free, is clear enough: imagination is free in so far as under speculatively fictitious forms essential truth may be conveyed, e.g. the eternal perfection and omnipotence of God under the fictitious forms of the righteousness of a legislator and the efficiency of an administrator in issuing and supporting decrees concerning durational behaviour. Similarly, submission to commands promulgated by a venerated authority is free in so far as the authority is rightly venerated, i.e. so occupies the mind, by reason of its unique character[5] in respect of its virtue, practical wisdom, and self-devotion to the service of moral principles, as to embody for the agent the moral *exemplar* that his speculative impotence would otherwise conceal. The authority of the prophet or statesman or system of laws is thus a *delegate* authority, though the delegation is imaginationally implicit rather than intellectually explicit—the fruit of wonder or astonishment, rather than of speculative insight. Kant's claim that a moral authority can only be recognized as such by a

---

[1] See above, Ch. XI, ii, (2) and (3).   [2] See above, p. 141.
[3] *Tract. Theo.-Pol., xvii.*   [4] See above, pp. 93–5.   [5] *See Eth. III, lii, et Sch.*

comparison with our ideal of moral perfection[1] is thus, though too intellectually phrased, essentially valid. The freedom of sub-mission, i.e. obedience, to external authority lies, therefore, in the propriety of the imaginational delegation of this authority from the essential source of moral authority, the eternal *exemplar* of the finite agent; and this can only be certified by the enlighten-ment of the intellect, though it may be rendered 'evident' by the issues of imaginational experience. In actual experience, however, since the veneration springs from belief in the virtue and wisdom of the prophet or statesman, the delegation of authority is partly certified and partly 'evident'. Nevertheless, false prophets and mere politicians are often improperly venerated, and the obedi-ence accorded to these provides only an illusory moral freedom, i.e. a freedom devoted to the interests of bondage—a bondage even more destructive as parasitical on a higher freedom.

3. *Mutual Freedom or Love*

In considering the nature of free submission or obedience, the relation of the subject to the ruler in the moralized civic State, or of the disciple to the prophet, has been chiefly in view rather than that of the ruler and the prophet to the subject and disciple respectively. But the ruler and the prophet, after all, are also men, and moral agents, and their relations with their subjects and disciples cannot be *altogether* other than those which we have considered. The distinction must be one of emphasis, by which a common relation is differentiated—the mutual relations of individual men being, in general, variations upon a universal theme according to the relative potencies which in them are available.

We saw[2] that in the eternal *Natura naturata* there is perfect community of all finite agents as infinitely graded finite actu-alizations of the primordial potency-in-act, so that the actual being of each lies in its community with its congruent comple-ment, and each is related to each by a true, or 'intellectual', love (as distinct from a love which is 'imaginational', and thus en-deavours after a return of love[3]). Now morality is the more or less partial approximation to this relation, *sub specie durationis*, under the 'emendation of the intellect', so that the general relation of

---

[1] See above, p. 142, note 1.   [2] See above, Ch. III.   [3] *Eth. V, xix.*

moral agents, as morally good, is one of durational sodality, variously differentiated according to their relative potencies or status. It is thus that, as we have seen,[1] 'mutual ethics' is the *proper* expression of 'exemplary ethics' under the conditions of multiplex unilateral finite self-reference, and not its *more expedient* substitute.

The nature of the freedom which ethical mutuality involves can thus be inferred as a privation of the derivative 'free necessity' of the eternal finite agents, which is actual as involving community with a complement which for each includes the other, under the 'free necessity' of eternal creation. It consists in the establishment of co-operation by the mutual adaptation of self and other in accordance with their relative status or potency. Where the relative status is that of more or less bounden agent and delegate *exemplar*, i.e. of subject and ruler, or disciple and prophet, it consists in free submission, or obedience, on the one hand, and on the other, moral cultivation, or enfranchizement, within the 'rampart' of civility; where it is that of a more perfect, i.e. free, agent and a less perfect, i.e. more bounden, agent, it consists in mutual adaptation in inverse proportion to perfection or freedom; and where the relation is between equals, it consists in mutual love or co-operative harmony.

Viewed from this standpoint, the scope of morality is indefinitely amplified so as to include the relations, not only of men with men, but also of men with superior and inferior agents. Of superior finite beings we have no knowledge, and man's relation with God has been, and will be further, considered elsewhere, but man's relation with inferior beings may be exemplified by the relations of the craftsman with his tools and materials, of the farmer with his beasts and crops and land, and the orator with his audience. The good craftsman so adapts his tools as to be extensions of his body, and the movements of both according to the nature of the material that he seeks to adapt to his purpose. The behaviour of the good farmer is adapted to the requirements of his beasts and crops and land, for only so will they respond to his requirements. And he is a sorry orator who seeks to move his audience without having regard to their passions, dispositions, and aspirations. So also with the moral relations of men: if the ruler or prophet is to obtain that obedience in the subject or

[1] Ch. X, ii, (1).

disciple which alone can stabilize his authority, he must promulgate his laws or teachings in a form suited to the prevailing natures of his subjects or disciples; the more mature and moralized parent or guardian must train and nurture his child or ward, not as if he were an equal, a brute, or a 'thing', but as one capable of adaptation to a more mature and moralized state; and the essence of the friendship of equals is reciprocal adaptation to a common life.

In general, that which renders the mind more understanding, and the body more physically effective, renders the whole man more free; and the mind becomes more understanding as it comes to know itself as the idea of a body the nature of which is not alien to its environment, but is 'affected' by it in many ways (and in eternal essence *constituted* by its community with its congruent complement): 'That which so disposes the human body that it can be affected in many ways, or which renders it capable of affecting external bodies in many ways, is profitable to man; and is more profitable in proportion as by its means the body becomes better fitted to be affected in many ways, and to affect other bodies.'[1] Thus, just as the 'free necessity' of the eternal finite agent is community, or mutual 'intellectual', or true, love, so the freedom of the durational finite conator is mutual 'imaginational' love among equals, and this modalized in accordance with relative status among unequals. For the true profit of both self and other lies in appropriate mutual adaptation; and where the agents are unequal in potency or freedom, the initiative belongs to the more active or superior: to the craftsman rather than the tool or material. And these are the principles more or less explicitly exemplified in what Spinoza has to say in *Part IV* of the *Ethics* about the man who lives in accordance with the dictates of reason?

II. 'FREE NECESSITY': ETERNAL 'BLESSEDNESS', AND THE 'INTELLECTUAL LOVE OF GOD'

'God or Nature', as perfectly active in self-acquiescent creativity, is perfectly free, i.e. *Natura naturans* eternally actualized as *Natura naturata*, the infinite macrocosm of finite microcosms of every grade of perfection, and in perfect constitutive, and therefore indivisible, community, acts by 'free necessity'—'free'

[1] *Eth. IV, xxxviii.*

because self-actualizing; 'necessary' because the actuality spring-ing, as such, from the primordial potency-in-act, is by this determined. And though the microcosms, as individual agents, are derivative, yet the 'free necessity' of the infinite 'whole' is imma-nent in them. For they are not mere *sectors* of the macrocosm, more or less extrinsically determined by their context of sectors but individual agents actualizing their own derivative finite potencies which, as co-derivative with the potencies of all finites, are actualized in eternal community with all.

This is the world as eternally created; the durational world is this eternal world as 'projected' upon the 'reference system' of the finite agent, and thus suffering the privation of potency that is *conatus*, and of actual existence that is duration; and the 'com-mon order of nature' is the integration of the many durational worlds of related finite agents—an integration which stems de-fectively from the community of *Natura naturata*. The moral order is the movement from privation to fulfilment by the correc-tion of self-reference, i.e. the 'emendation of the intellect' in both self and other under the *nisus* of eternity that remains under finite self-reference according to the variant status of the finite individuals. For each durational agent has its roots in eternity—is in part eternal and in part durational, since the more perfectly in its eternal nature it actualizes the infinite primordial potency, the less it suffers privation under self-reference. *Natura naturata* itself is at once self-referent and 'referred to God'; the *modus simplicissimus* would, by self-reference, be so debilitated as to be reduced to near nonentity; and between these limits lies the sphere of morality with its bifurcated causality and elective actuality.

Now, the life of moral virtue is one of effective joyful endeavour after what is truly profitable. The free man 'endeavours as much as possible to do well and rejoice',[1] and eternal life is the life of which this is the durational privation at its best, viz. the 'blessed-ness' of perfect eternal agency. For the *affectus* of joy is privative in so far as it is the idea of a transition concomitant with *affectio* by another, by association with the idea of which, love for the other is constituted. Yet this 'love' is 'imaginational', and thus a privation of true, or 'intellectual', love, which springs from no *affectio*, but from the immanence of its 'object' in the very agency

[1] *Eth. IV, l, Sch.; lxxiii, Sch.*

of the self. And what 'joy' is to imaginational 'love', 'blessedness' is to true, or 'intellectual' love, i.e. to perfect understanding by the 'third kind of knowledge'. 'Joy' is the confused summary idea of appraisement of the transition to a greater perfection, but 'blessedness' is the tranquil possession by the mind of its proper perfection: 'if joy consist in the passage to a greater perfection, blessedness must indeed consist in this, that the mind is endowed with perfection itself'.[1] And this eternal tranquillity of mind[2] is possible for the finite agent only 'as referred to God', so that it thus constitutes the 'intellectual love of God', which in its fullness is proper to God alone, who 'loves himself with an infinite intellectual love',[3] delighting in the infinite actual perfection of which his infinite potency-in-act is the cause. Yet the finite agent, as eternal *creatum* delights also in his finite perfection as derived from, and referred to, God, so that his 'intellectual love towards God is part of the infinite love with which God loves himself'— is, indeed, 'the very love with which God loves himself, not in so far as he is infinite, but in so far as he can be manifested through the essence of the human mind considered *sub specie aeternitatis*'.[4] In his love for himself is involved God's love for men, but that love is 'intellectual' and not 'imaginational': it involves no transition in the nature of God to a greater perfection by the service of men, but is a 'part' of his perfection—so that 'he who loves God cannot strive that God should love him in return',[5] i.e. with an 'imaginational' love. For if he loves God truly, i.e. intellectually, that love itself is God's love for him, and is thus its own 'return', and no extrinsic reward for service.

Further, since 'blessedness' is possible only as all things are 'referred to God', it is one with the intellectual love of God, and no mere imaginational association of an *affectus* with an idea of its cause, as with imaginational joy and love. Thus, Spinoza is able to identify 'blessedness' with virtue itself. It is not the reward of virtue, but the intrinsic possession of the virtuous agent—is, indeed, the very motive of virtuous action, since it is our delight in it that enables us to restrain our lusts.[6] Blessedness is the very power of the emended intellect, by which we are able, in so far as we understand the natures of 'self and God and things' by the 'third kind of knowledge', to 'do well and rejoice'

---

[1] *Eth. V, xxxiii, Sch.*   [2] '*Acquiescentia in se ipso.*'   [3] *Eth. V, xxxv.*
[4] *Eth. V, xxxvi.*   [5] *Eth. V, xix.*   [6] *Eth. V, xlii.*

sub specie durationis, with a 'joy continuous and supreme for eternity'.[1] For even *sub specie durationis,* eternal blessedness is not postponed to a supposed life *after* death, but may irradiate the very 'now' of action. For 'this present life' is not *other* than eternity, but its *privation,* in which finiteness spells duration, and otherness mortality. Man's immortality lies in his eternity as *creatum,* and not in durational persistence, or an after-life. It lies *perdue* in the continuant 'now' of endeavour, because the 'now' of endeavour is its durational efflux, and is durational only as the efflux of eternity. If human liberation were solely dependent on durational human effort (as the humanists contend), it would be impossible; if it were a divine gift involving only submission under pain of sanction to divine command (as theologians have sometimes held), morality would be superfluous, or at best degraded to expediency; but because liberation is exemplary intellectual self-emendation, or, where intellectual gift is lacking, obedience to a delegate *exemplar,* and in either case under immanent and congruent divine *nisus,* it is universally available, difficult, and momentous. 'If the way which leads hither seem very difficult, it can nevertheless be found. It must indeed be difficult since it is so seldom discovered; for if salvation lay ready to hand, and could be found without great labour, how could it be possible that it should be neglected by nearly all? But all things excellent are as difficult as they are rare.'[2]

[1] *Tract. de Intell. Emend.,* § 1.   [2] *Eth. V, xlii, Sch.*

M

INDEX

I. REFERENCES TO THE WORKS OF SPINOZA

II. SUBJECTS, PERSONAL NAMES, AND CATCHWORDS

166 INDEX